THE HUGH MACDIARMID–
GEORGE OGILVIE
LETTERS

the Hugh MacDiarmid-George Ogilvie letters

edited by

Catherine Kerrigan

ABERDEEN UNIVERSITY PRESS

First published 1988
The Aberdeen University Press
A member of the Pergamon Group

British Library Cataloguing in Publication Data

MacDiarmid, Hugh, *1892–1978*
 The Hugh MacDiarmid–George Ogilvie letters
 1. Poetry in English. MacDiarmid, Hugh,
 1892–1978—Correspondence, diaries, etc.
 Rn: Christopher Murray Grieve I. Title
 II. Ogilvie, George III. Kerrigan, Catherine
 821'.912

 ISBN 0 08 036409 8

This book has been published with the help of a grant from the
Canadian Federation for the Humanities,
using funds provided by the
Social Sciences and Humanities Research Council of Canada,

PRINTED IN GREAT BRITAIN
THE UNIVERSITY PRESS
ABERDEEN

CONTENTS

LIST OF ILLUSTRATIONS

PREFACE AND ACKNOWLEDGEMENTS

This collection of letters from Christopher Murray Grieve to George Ogilvie was kept in Ogilvie's possession until close to his death in 1934. At that time, Ogilvie passed the letters on to another teacher at Broughton, J G Sinclair. It seems to have been the plan that Sinclair would annotate and publish the letters, but he never completed the task and the letters were later given to James King Annand, who was also an old Broughtonian. In 1968 Annand published the poems which had accompanied the letters under the title, *Hugh MacDiarmid: Early Lyrics*, and in the introduction to that work quoted extensively from the letters. Subsequent to this, the collection was acquired by the National Library of Scotland where it is presently housed.

This edition includes several letters from Ogilvie to MacDiarmid which were donated to Edinburgh University Library by the Grieve family after the poet's death. One additional letter from the poet to Ogilvie and an early prose piece, *Casualties*, both of which were first published in *Broughton Magazine*, have been included. Enquiries have failed to produce any further letters from Ogilvie and as a result the correspondence as a whole is one-sided.

MacDiarmid was a prolific writer and the letters to Ogilvie constitute only a small part of his enormous output, but the correspondence is of special importance because it contains the earliest surviving letters and is therefore a valuable source of information on the poet's early life. The early work of any writer is highly significant for the picture it gives of the writer's development, and this is no less so in MacDiarmid's case. The correspondence gives a very striking picture of a literary talent in embryo. At the same time, the letters also chronicle MacDiarmid's responses to a world of rapidly changing political and social structures, and it is clear that for MacDiarmid the literary and the political were always intertwined.

MacDiarmid certainly made his mark on the literary and political scene in the twenties and thirties and to this day remains the most important single influence on Scottish culture. The letters document his struggles and successes in that period and provide a history of the roots and development of the early modern revival. If in making this correspondence available in the present format this volume contributes to an enlarged understanding of both the man and the motives of the modern Scottish cultural revival then it will have played its part.

This project was begun before Alan Bold announced his intention to produce a volume of MacDiarmid's *Collected Letters*. Although Mr Bold decided to include a considerable number of the letters to Ogilvie in his selection, the plan of the present volume pursues a different end. In order to give as full a picture as possible of MacDiarmid's early development, the correspondence has here been reproduced in its entirety and extensive notes giving detailed, verifiable information provided. This method was adopted, not only to help dissolve some of the myths which have accumulated around MacDiarmid's early life, but also to help illuminate the arena within which those events—and his writing—took place. MacDiarmid is a poet who cries out to be understood in context. That the context of his early life was also a great watershed in modern history makes it all the more important to have a fuller understanding of the relationship of his work to time and place.

Acknowledgements

Any edition of letters of a writer who is still very much a part of living memory owes an enormous debt to an army of individuals who gave of their time and energy in answering the editor's queries. My obligation in acknowledging this help is made all the more pleasant by the courtesy and enthusiasm so many individuals showed towards me and the project.

I should like to thank the trustees of the National Library of Scotland for giving me access to the MacDiarmid letters and to the trustees of Edinburgh University Library for extending the same privilege to the Ogilvie letters. But most of all I should like to thank Michael and Valda Grieve for permission to publish the collection. James King Annand gave a number of references and some history of the Broughton days. Broughton school kindly allowed me to reproduce material from their magazine. Morag Enticknap and Jean White (to whom I owe an apology for a mistake in her name in another work) supplied vital information on the Grieve family. Neil Evans, Dr Deian Hopkin, Dr Colin Holmes, Dr Kenneth O Morgan, Dr Hywel Francis, Cledwyn Fychan and Patricia Moore all tried valiantly to help me trace the missing *Monmouthsire Labour News*. Janet Adam Smith gave advice on trying to track down a missing correspondence between MacDiarmid and John Buchan and Dr Joanna Kitchin kindly supplied some information on her father. The staff of *Scotsman Publications*, *The Irish Times* and *Scottish Field*, assisted me in identifying reviews, people and events, as did the Scottish Education Department, The Ministry of Defence and other government agencies. Miles Marshall, the Haynes Publishing Group and Routledge and Kegan Paul all tried to trace the works MacDiarmid said he had placed with these publishers.

For expert advice and guidance I am once again indebted to Professor John MacQueen of the School of Scottish Studies for his ever-generous help and support and to Professor B Rajan of the University of Western Ontario for his assistance.

The research was financed jointly by 'A Thank Offering to Britain' from the British Academy and by the Social Sciences and Research Council of Canada and I would like to express my deep appreciation to both funding agencies.

As ever, the staff of the National Library of Scotland cannot be praised highly enough for the help they gave and similar thanks are due to Edinburgh University Library, particularly to Dr John Hall. Lastly, I would like to say thanks to my family and to colleagues at the School of Scottish Studies whose good-natured advice and tolerance are always a tonic.

Editorial Principles

The aim throughout has been to transcribe the original texts as faithfully as possible. MacDiarmid's script is very clear, with little illegibility, but where there is doubt this is indicated by the editor's question mark in square brackets, as are all editorial intrusions into the text itself. Omissions have been supplied but no alterations that would in any way change the meaning have been made. Although he regularly misspells proper names, generally, MacDiarmid's spelling is accurate. In the case of Scots words, these have been transcribed exactly as they appear in the text. Punctuation is often more dramatic than precise, but because this is integral to the style—particularly the frequent use of dashes and exclamation marks—the original has been preserved. Where questions do arise, the demands of the context have been met. Abbreviations have been allowed to stand, but 'and' replaces the ampersand throughout.

The bulk of the letters are dated in a precise manner, but occasionally only the day of the week, or sometimes simply the month or season of the year is given. Where possible specific dates have been supplied using internal evidence or external sources of information. Placing of undated letters in chronological order has been carried out, but all cases of indeterminate dating are indicated by a question mark. Postscripts and afterthoughts, wherever they occur in the text, have in transcription been placed at the end of the letter, following on the closing signature. The signature of each letter has been included because the variations in signatures carry their own special significance. MacDiarmid's original page numbers and library manuscript numbers have been omitted throughout.

This book has been published with the help of a grant from the Canadian Federation for the Humanities, using funds provided by the Social Sciences and Humanities Research Council of Canada.

CHRONOLOGY

1892
11 August Born at Arkinholm Terrace, Langholm.
1897 Enrolled in Langholm Infant School.
1899 Enrolled in the primary department of Langholm Academy. Family moved to house in the Library Buildings.
1904 Transferred to the secondary department of Langholm Academy.
1905 Teaching Bible Classes at Langholm South United Free Church.
1908 Admitted as a pupil teacher to Broughton Junior Student Centre in Edinburgh. Met Ogilvie. Joined the Edinburgh branch of the ILP and the Edinburgh University Branch of the Fabian Society.
1909–1910 Edited *Broughton Magazine*.
1911
3 February Father, James Grieve, died.
  Left Broughton and worked as a junior reporter on the *Edinburgh Evening Dispatch*.
11 July First article, 'The Young Astrology', published in *The New Age*.
? August Left Edinburgh and went to work in South Wales as a reporter with the *Monmouthshire Labour News*.
1912 Returned to Langholm. Moved to Clydebank to work on the *Clydebank and Renfrew Press*. Rejoined the ILP. Moved to Cupar to work for Innes Group of newspapers. Met Margaret Skinner.
1913 Moved to Forfar to work on the *Forfar Review*.
1915
June Enlisted.
1916
August Promoted to sergeant. Served with 42nd General Hospital RAMC in Salonika. Contracted malaria.
1918 Invalided home with malaria to a camp in Rhyl.
13 June Married Margaret Skinner.
November Posted to Sections Lahore Indian General Hospital near Marseilles.
1919 Demobbed.
  Joined his wife in St Andrews, found a job with the *Montrose Review* and moved to Montrose.

1920

6 October   Moved to Kildermorie, Easter Ross, to take up a post as a teacher.

November   *Northern Numbers (First Series)*

1921

26 April   Resigned post at Kildermorie and returned to Montrose to work once again on the *Montrose Review*.

October   *Northern Numbers* (Second Series)

1922   Moved to house at 16 Links Avenue, Montrose.

August   *Scottish Chapbook*

December   *Northern Numbers* (Third Series)

1923   Joined P.E.N. International

8 May   *Scottish Nation*

      Annals of the Five Senses

1924

May   *Northern Review*

4 September   First child, Christine, born.

1925   Applied unsuccessfully for the post of Keeper at the National Gallery of Scotland.

9 September   *Sangschaw*

1926   Appointed Justice of the Peace in Montrose.

10 June   *Penny Wheep*

26 November   *A Drunk Man Looks at the Thistle*

      Contemporary Scottish Studies

      Robert Burns (Augustan Book of Poetry Series)

1927   *The Lucky Bag*

      Albyn: or Scotland and the Future

1928

5 April   Second child, Walter, born.

23 June   Founder member of the National Party of Scotland.

1929   Moved to London to edit *Vox*.

1930   Moved to Liverpool to work as public relations officer.

      To Circumjack Cencrastus

1931   Returned to London.

      First Hymn to Lenin

1932   Divorced from Margaret Skinner.

      Moved to Thakeham, Surrey, with Valda Trevlyn

      Second Hymn to Lenin

      Living Scottish Poets

      Scots Unbound

28 July   Third child, Michael, born. Returned to Scotland and lived at Longniddry.

1933   Moved to Whalsay in Shetland.

ABBREVIATIONS

A.F.S.	*Annals of the Five Senses*
C.K.	*The Company I've Kept*
C.P.	*The Complete Poems. 2 Vols.*
C.S.S.	*Contemporary Scottish Studies*
L.P.	*Lucky Poet*
N.N.	*Northern Numbers. Series 1, 2 and 3*
N.R.	*Northern Review*
S.C.	*Scottish Chapbook*
S.E.	*Selected Essays*
S.N.	*Scottish Nation*

INTRODUCTION

In 1911 the young Christopher Murray Grieve began a correspondence with his former teacher, George Ogilvie, a correspondence which was to continue until shortly before Ogilvie's death in the early thirties. Ogilvie obviously treasured the letters, for he carefully saved them. He must have felt at a very early date that there was somthing quite extraordinary in the writing and confidences of this unusual student of his, and he was right. The awkward literary trials and errors of young Grieve were later to flower into the lyric outpourings of Hugh MacDiarmid and the first signs of this great poetic voice surfaced in these early letters.

George Ogilvie was MacDiarmid's English teacher at Broughton Junior Student Centre in Edinburgh, the school where MacDiarmid had gone to train as a teacher in 1908. MacDiarmid formed a very strong attachment to Ogilvie, a surprising fact, for the two men were opposites. Ogilvie was a shy school master, a pillar of support to his students, but self-effacing about his own accomplishments. MacDiarmid was a boisterous, uncontrollable energy, constantly swinging between the poles of exultation and despair, arrogant in his successes and vindictive towards those he saw as enemies of his purpose. Yet, a genuine friendship developed between the two. The letters reveal MacDiarmid's deep respect and fondness for Ogilvie, feelings which continued throughout his life, while the few letters from Ogilvie which have survived, show a remarkable sensitivity towards a young writer who was often difficult and demanding.

Not a great deal is known about George Ogilvie. The little information which has emerged comes mainly from recollections and tributes by former students and colleagues. In one of these he is described as

> . . . slightly below middle height, slimly yet wirily built. His eyes were brown and kindly; and his curious habit of keeping them half closed when speaking gave a curious apologetic and abstracted manner, save with his intimates, he seemed rather nervous and diffident; and his speech was often punctuated by a short, dry, nervous cough. In dress he usually wore grey, sometimes middle, sometimes dark. In winter he wore a grey-toned cardigan. For headgear he almost invariable wore a bowler which, slightly tilted over one eyebrow and precariously rather than firmly seated on his head, gave a slight touch of insouciance to his appearance. His voice was rather soft and husky with the suspicion of a burr and a slight west-country lilt in it.[1]

Photographs of Ogilvie bear out this description and the tilt of his bowler hat and the humour in his lively eyes give the impression of wit and good temper, qualities which MacDiarmid felt were a part of Ogilvie's great personal attractiveness.

George Ogilvie at Broughton School.

George Ogilvie was born in Glasgow in 1871. His mother died when George was still an infant, and his father, John, an engineer, took the family to live in his native Kilmarnock. There the family was brought up by the maternal grandmother and the children were educated at the local school. When he had finished his schooling, Ogilvie was apprenticed as a draughtsman to an engineering works. George Ogilvie's background, like MacDiarmid's, was one of evangelism, and in 1899, spurred on by the visit of the American preachers, Moody and Sankey, he joined the Kilmarnock Christian Union, became president of its Young Men's Fellowship, and took to preaching in the streets. It was during this period of intense religious commitment that Ogilvie decided to train for the Ministry, and in 1894 he took the entrance examination for Glasgow University. But at university his direction changed to an interest in literature, perhaps because he had several outstanding teachers, among them the Shakespearian critic, A C Bradley, and the classicist, Gilbert Murray. Graduating in 1899 with English honours, Ogilvie was awarded the John Clarke Scholarship. He subsequently took teacher training and, after completing his studies, had a series of appointments in Glasgow and Fife, until in 1904, he went to Broughton as head teacher of the English Department.

The year Ogilvie arrived at Broughton the school was being transformed into a higher grade centre of education which, while continuing with teacher education, would also prepare students for university entrance. When in 1907 the institution completed its reorganisation, the curriculum had been greatly expanded to include the Liberal Arts subjects—English, Languages, Maths, Science, History, Classics, Geography and Art—and the new staff (mainly young university graduates) were better suited than their predecessors to meet the ideals of the new Education Acts.

A committed teacher, Ogilvie seemed respected by all who knew him. At Broughton he formed a Literary Society, a Drama Club, and launched the school magazine. *Broughton Magazine* was less a news-sheet for recording the usual school trivia than a genuine attempt to provide a platform for those with literary abilities, and its success can be measured by the fact that a number of its student editors went on to pursue, in one form or another, a career in writing. MacDiarmid edited the school magazine in 1910, and contributed various short stories, prose pieces and a few poems, all very much the work of an adolescent, but energetic in a way which distinguishes them from other contributions. The school magazine was where MaDiarmid first exercised his literary muscle, and that he always held a deep affection for it tells in the way in which he eagerly responded to Ogilvie's requests for contributions over the years.

On his first day at Broughton, MacDiarmid made an immediate impression on Ogilvie.

> I remember vividly Grieve's arrival amongst us. I see the little slimly built figure in hodden grey, the sharp-featured face with its piercing eyes, the striking head with its broad brow and great mass of flaxen curly hair. He hailed from Langholm, and had a Border accent you could cut with a knife. I am afraid some of the city students smiled at first at the newcomer, but he very speedily won their respect. He certainly very quickly established himself in mine. His first essay (an unseen done in class) is still to my mind the finest bit of work I have got in Broughton. The subject was 'A

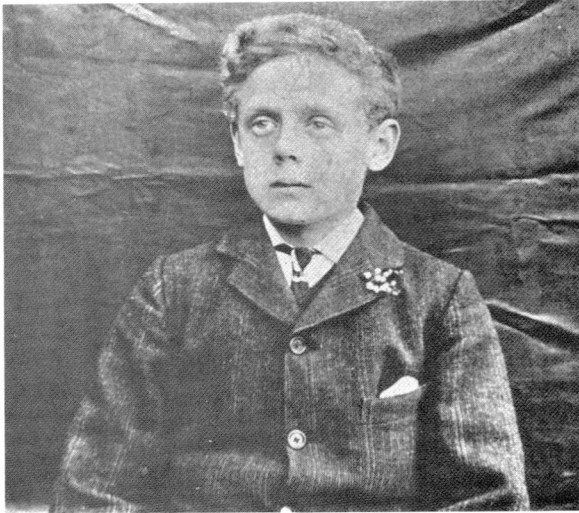

MacDiarmid when he was aged about eleven.

MacDiarmid in his late 'teens.

Country Road', and Grieve hedged it with wayside beauty and paved it with the golden romances of the Borders. You may be sure that I made it my chief business from that day on to keep my eye on Grieve. He did not belie the promise of his early start.[2]

Ogilvie gave MacDiarmid a great deal of encouragement in his early years, and that he had the power to fire the young man's imagination tells in MacDiarmid's references to Ogilvie's 'kindling power', part of which stemmed from the teacher's ability to awaken interest in the native literary tradition which, then as now, was not a mandatory subject in Scottish classrooms.

Ogilvie had distinct socialist leanings. As a student in Glasgow he had worked at one of the Settlement Houses in a slum district, living with the poor and ministering to more than their spiritual needs. MacDiarmid described Ogilvie as a 'quiet revolutionary', one of those human beings who change circumstances by private acts of courage and compassion. MacDiarmid wrote that Ogilvie's socialism 'sprang from the heart. . . . He believed that we are all made of the same common clay, and that good men may become evil in certain circumstances and that evil men may be uplifted.'[3] Whether or not Ogilvie, like MacDiarmid, actually joined any socialist group is not known, but he certainly must have been receptive to the movement, for it is unlikely that MacDiarmid would have written to him so enthusiastically about his early political successes had the case been otherwise.

At Broughton, academic standards were high, but the atmosphere was generally informal and school life had a whole social dimension. MacDiarmid played an active part in school events. He made many friends there and throughout the years of his correspondence with Ogilvie there are constant references to and enquiries about the health and welfare of his old schoolmates. MacDiarmid was happy at Broughton, and even although he left the school without any academic qualifications, and under a cloud of suspicion, his fond memories of those years are conveyed in the letters.

MacDiarmid's break with school and personal contact with Ogilvie came in the year the correspondence started. In February 1911, MacDiarmid was peripherally involved in the theft of some of Ogilvie's books and his part in the offence was about to be investigated when he officially withdrew from the centre. At the time his father was seriously ill, so it was probably the combination of the two sets of circumstances which forced him to leave. His father died, and after a brief spell as a reporter on an Edinburgh newspaper, MacDiarmid left for Wales. It was from Wales that he wrote the earliest surviving letter to Ogilvie.

Thus, the correspondence began with a crisis, a pattern which was to repeat itself over the years. The first letter tells of MacDiarmid's 'mental and moral anarchy', the large childish hand in which it is written betrays his immaturity, and the tone tells of his need to find a replacement for his dead father. That George Ogilvie responded quickly and compassionately to such a desperate *cri de coeur* reveals those qualities in his character which MacDiarmid was to rely on for many years to come.

Very little is known about MacDiarmid's time in Wales—why he went there,

C. M. GRIEVE.

EDWARD ALBERT, M.A.

Capt. A. B. DURWARD, M.A.
(*Killed in Action*)

R. W. KERR, M.A.

A. D. MACKIE, M.A.

MacDiarmid (C M Grieve) with some of the fellow Broughtonians mentioned in the letters.

J. G. SINCLAIR
General Editor, 1921-

C. M. GRIEVE
Editor, 1909-1910

G. OGILVIE
Founder and General Editor, 1907-1921

J. D. KENNEDY,
Art Master, 1938-1956

MacDiarmid with some of the masters of Broughton School and editors of the school
magazine.

who secured the job for him, what political movements he was actually involved in, etc—so that this period presents a large gap in his history. MacDiarmid wrote to Ogilvie about his work as a reporter on the *Monmouthshire Labour News*, giving details of the civil unrest that was then taking place in South Wales, and this information is in itself valuable social history. According to his own description of the situation, MacDiarmid was in the thick of the disturbances:

> Did you see any account of the recent pogroms in Bargod, Tredegar, Rhymney, Ebbw Vale and Cum? They gave me my first taste of war corresponding and I narrowly escaped being bludgeoned more than once. I heard the Riot Act read thrice in one night (in different towns, of course) and saw seventeen baton charges. My attack on the police, for their conduct during these riots, sent up the sales of the paper considerably. I did not get to bed for four consecutive nights and was the only reporter at the meeting of the rioters . . . my editor thought fit to warn me that in all probability I would be arrested for aiding and abetting.
>
> (24 October 1911)

The graphic description of events suggests the quality of MacDiarmid's reporting, and while 'pogroms' may be too strong a word to describe the element of anti-Jewish feeling in some of the riots, his account of the situation is accurate and has recently been supported by the research of historians.[4]

MacDiarmid's journalistic attacks on the police and local authorities, his penchant for writing 'extremist articles' was, however, to bring him into confrontation with the local seats of power. He told Ogilvie that although he had been 'delightfully immersed in labour movement', and as an ardent supporter of the ILP had helped to form four new branches in South Wales, he suddenly found himself 'shipwrecked on hidden rocks of implacable liberalism and non-conformity in bright seas of labourist activity'. The content of the offending articles is not described, but given MacDiarmid's temperament, they probably contained criticism of local public leaders. Not given to compromise, even at that tender age, he was 'horribly unrepentant and truculent', interpreting attempts at at conciliation as 'species of hypocrisy attributable to the partial development of too generous ideals in unsuitable natures'. If the articles contained invective like this, it is little wonder that when the newspaper reorganised, the inevitable happened.

After his stay in Wales, MacDiarmid returned to Scotland and worked for the next few years on a series of local newspapers. He seems initially to have thoroughly enjoyed the bustling life of a reporter, for it brought him into contact with a wide range of experiences and many 'boon companions' whose 'libations were limitless'. But, as he explained to Ogilvie, after a time he saw that he had to break the pattern of his life. He kept his job, but took a cottage in the country with his mother as housekeeper, an arrangement which kept him from the excesses of conviviality and allowed him to pursue his real work, 'what I am pleased to consider my life-work'.

Unfortunately, this quiet spell of purposeful writing was to be short-lived. War was declared and it rapidly became impossible 'for a young man physically fit to remain in "civies"'. A reluctant soldier, MacDiarmid, against the odds, had a fairly successful time in the army. It may be that he benefited from the imposed discipline of army life, for he wrote of his life as a soldier with some pride, qualified however by some self-deprecating humour:

> Within six months of joining I had risen from a recruit to be Acting Quarter-Master-Sergeant of a Company 1000 strong. I had acquired not only discipline, a certain mastery of and confidence in myself, and a command of men, but a sense of responsibility, a certain business ability, and the habit of being trusted and trustworthy. . . . In full rig-out with sling-sword belt, and polished crowns, and knee-breeches and tan boots, I was 'some nut' too. . . .
>
> (20 August 1916)

MacDiarmid's war records have not survived, they were destroyed in a blitz during the Second World War, so the history of his army days, like his time in Wales, rests heavily on the accounts he gave in his letters to Ogilvie.

The bulk of MacDiarmid's army service was carried out in Salonika where he served with the Royal Army Medical Corps. In Greece the situation was tense. After mobilisation, Greece had requested Allied troops to aid in the defence of Serbia, but when they arrived King Constantine promptly declared Greece neutral. The Allied position was thus very precarious, and was made even more difficult by the fact that the British and French commanders were at odds with each other, the forces were under constant bombardment from air-raids and the soldiers were devasted by malaria and dysentery.

MacDiarmid's first letter from Salonika hints at the political situation there, but because of censorship, his comments were confined to a description of his duties:

> The Sergeant-Caterer of the Officers' Mess (that's my new post in our little military world here) has to go 'on deck' at dinner—dinner commencing 7.30p.m. and running to some five courses—freshly shaven, boots and buttons mirror-bright, properly dressed with belt and all. He does nothing of course, save supervision. A spot of tarnish on a knife or fork—lack-lustre of a wine-glass—uneven flaming of one of the hanging lamps—slackness on the part of the waiters—slow, slovenly, or uneven dishing-up on the part of the cooks—what an eye one develops for detail on such a job! Between the Mess-Marquée, and the Mess cook-house, is a strip of open hillside over which the waiters run backwards and forwards in the moony Macedonian night. Brightly the beams fall on platefuls of white vegetable soup, patum peperium entrées, portions of cottage pie enlivened with rice-stuffed peppers, liberal helpings of rice and raisins, coffee-pots—and later when the Mess has come to the walnuts and almonds and the wine steward is busy supplying Vin Blanc, Vin Russe, or vin Muscat de Samos . . . the Sergeant-Caterer and his staff dine too. (What an awful war, to be sure!).
>
> (20 August 1916)

Life in Salonika was obviously slow and tedious but it did give MacDiarmid time to read and write. However, writing did not come easily. MacDiarmid wanted to capture the experience of the war, but he felt overwhelmed by the

MacDiarmid with his mother. Taken during the First World War.

chaos of events, a feeling he gave expression to in 'A Four Years' Harvest', an early prose piece:

> He found it impossible to express, even with any minimum of intelligibility, his consuming sense of the utter and impermissible estrangement of practically all that had been spoken or written—thought was perhaps another matter!—about the war from the facts as he had seen them . . .—or to indicate the cause of the desperate and agonising impotence that seized him whenever he was constrained . . . to consider the ways and means by which his experiences might ever become even in the remotest degree—no, not acceptable—but merely expressible. So great was the conspiracy of misunderstanding that even general knowledge (to soldiers) on various aspects of the subject was as incapable of proof, or citation (to non-soldiers), as the history of a new dimension.
>
> (in *Annals of the Five Senses*, pp 61–103)

The sense that it was not possible to capture in writing the panorama of events, the sense that experience had become hopelessly fragmented, was the demon MacDiarmid wrestled with during these war years, and he saw that others were faced with the same difficulty:

> He had waded through Mr Bernard Shaw's harangues, Mr Arnold Bennett's reply and Shaw's rebuttal. He had listened to Mr Hilaire Belloc's world without end. He had seen it through with Mr Britling. Mr Rider Haggard's articles had excited his ghastly amusement, and Mr Harold Begbie's nerve-shattering detestation. Dr Dernberg and Count von Bernstoff had not been lost on him. And he had read and reread *Germany and the Next War*, and those splendid books, Professor Cramb's *Germany and England*, and *The New Map of Europe*, by Professor Gibbons. Dr Armgaard Karl Graves had not been overlooked, nor had the countless letters to the press, which had added to the weirdness and mysteries of life. And he had heard Mr Lloyd George passionately aver at Bwyfdle that this war, like the next war, is a war to end war.
>
> ('A Four Years' Harvest')

MacDiarmid saw the difficulty of trying to seize with any degree of truth or accuracy the complexity of the situation and recognised the bewilderment of the major writers of the day as they struggled to express events in an idiom which no longer served the purpose.

Towards the close of the war, in November 1918, MacDiarmid was transferred to France. During his time in Salonika he had suffered badly from malaria and was now being sent, first, to a camp 'in the area of Dieppe', and then to a large hospital for Indian soldiers in Marseilles. Arriving in France shortly before Armistice Day, MacDiarmid witnessed the aftermath of the Battle of the Somme and in response wrote a short prose piece which was later published by Ogilvie in the school magazine. The ending of 'Casualties' tells of MacDiarmid's reaction to the torn landscape of battle:

> Up to that ridge wandered the indescribable waste of the countryside, trenched and pitted and ploughed until it had become a fantastic and nightmarish wilderness. On this dreary tract nothing remained of the gifts once showered by nature. But the grim legacies of man at war were countless—chaotic and half-buried heaps of

machinery, munitions, equipment, and the remains of his hasty meals. And he himself lay there, shattered in thousands, to give lurking horror to a treacherous and violent surface of mud and slime and unlovely litter. The very weeds which might have graced the desolation refused such holding-ground.

Pale now beside the compelling splendour of reddening day showed the yellow stabs of our guns, flashes that had lit the sky in the night watches, and only the long road, never varying, told that the unspeakable harvest on the Somme was still being gathered in.

(*Broughton Magazine*, Summer 1919, pp 15–17)

The above lines convey MacDiarmid's sense of the utter futility of war. War is inglorious death, apocalyptic destruction, the severing of the links between the human and the natural worlds. Like his contemporary Siegfried Sassoon, MacDiarmid recognised that a war which ostensibly had begun as one of defence, had followed the path of all wars and ended in aggression, slaughter and conquest.

When the termination of hostilities was announced on 11 November, MacDiarmid wrote of the troops' reaction to the news, 'It was taken very, very quietly—incalculable relief, but no mafficking.' In response to Ogilvie's celebration of the Allied victory, he replied, 'I myself believe that we have lost this war—in everything but actuality! When I see scores of sheep go to a slaughter house I do not feel constrained to admire their resignation . . .' (24 November 1918).

MacDiarmid predicted that post-war Britain would witness a major reconstruction of social and class values. The revolution in Russia was a sign that world-wide changes were underway. He was getting news of the labour troubles on Clydeside and was eager to be out of the army and back in the thick of the labour movement: 'Exciting rumours of industrial happenings are trickling through—I wonder what's what really, and, if there is to be anything really *big* doing, cannot imagine how I will support existence away here out of it all . . .' (23 March 1919). But it was to be some months yet before MacDiarmid was demobbed, time he filled by writing to Ogilvie of his literary experiments and plans.

The lengthy letters which MacDiarmid wrote to Ogilvie during his army years are among the most intense of the whole correspondence, for these letters convey very strongly the sense of a young writer trying to find himself. Plagued by spells of doubt and depression, MacDiarmid relied on Ogilvie's constant encouragement and reassurance. He desperately wanted to write something which would meet with Ogilvie's approval, but as the time lapses between the letters suggest, he could not produce at will. Periods of silence would be followed by letters describing the 'psychological tangle from which I have never freed myself'. There are references to his sense of warring personalities which 'stultify each other' and of his 'unspeakable relief' when he received Ogilvie's reassurances.

As a possible remedy to his sense of thwarted creativity, Ogilvie suggested to MacDiarmid that he write a 'psychological history'. MacDiarmid obliged, but what he wrote was more a potted autobiography (the letter of 20 August 1916), giving a chronological sequence of events in his life in the days before he joined the army. However, within months he was writing excitedly about 'a trilogy of autobiographic novels' which he described as 'somewhat of a cross between Gorki's *Childhood* and Wells's *Tono-Bungay*' (4 December 1917). Like so many of the early works MacDiarmid refers to in these letters, it is difficult to determine whether he actually wrote this work, or whether he had simply put together some notes (he does refer to work of this date being in 'rough draft'). It seems likely that some of this work was incorporated into what was later published as *Annals of the Five Senses*, for by December 1918 he was telling Ogilvie that he was 'busily licking into shape . . . . a sheaf of studies similar in angle of approach to 'Cerebral' but dealing with diverse psychological crises and reactions', a description which fits the contents of *Annals*.

MacDiarmid confessed that he wrote pieces like 'Cerebral' after bouts of 'neuritis', but that he had learned to deal with these periods of acute depression by 'using my natural safety valve', that is, by writing. 'Cerebral' itself is a description of the mind of a writer who (like the young James Joyce) wants to write on Ibsen and is tracing the Scottish element in the dramatist's work, and visualising himself as the 'Ibsen of Edinburgh'. MacDiarmid's piece is an attempt to combine Ibsen's psychological depth with a Dostoevskian surrealistic self-awareness:

> . . . he would suddenly see his brain as a writhing mass of worms. One part would beat like a pulse, growing louder and louder—swell enormously—then burst, deluging his mind in warm blood. He was obsessed—then recovering from the terrible phantasy, nerveless and blanched, he would watch with painful realism the break-up of his mental life. Every one of his separate egos became violently anarchical, creating an unthinkable Babel. Disunity and internecine hostility tore him into shreds. This passing, he would darken into lethargy, thus eventually recovering his poise in sleep, and the memories of such crises were almost indistinguishable from nightmares.
>
> (in *Annals of the Five Senses*, pp 21–34)

The acute self-exploration seen in the above, and in similar works, was described by MacDiarmid as 'mystical psychoanalysis', and he told Ogilvie that he had written a series of ten volumes, 'over 100 stories in all', in that style. If that is the case, very little of this work was ever published, and it is doubtful that much of it has survived.

Writing in this vein seems to have effected some kind of release for MacDiarmid, for there then followed a period of 'mental spate' and he sent to Ogilvie long lists and descriptions of work in progress. There are references to a 'Henry Jamesy' novel, a 'study of the technique and temper of Joseph Conrad's work', an essay on Futurism which he would have sent to *Blast* if it were still in circulation, several sonnet sequences, a series of 'Catholic adventures', numerous articles on Scottish writers and Scottish subjects, a Parisian sketch designed for the back pages of the *Manchester Guardian*, a series of 'post-war essays, psychological in intent', a '20,000 word "book" on "The Soviet State"', a volume of literary criticism, and much more. MacDiarmid's habit of reworking and retitling (not to mention his often extensive plagiarisms) makes it difficult to pinpoint the place of this early work in his later publications. Add to that the fact that MacDiarmid would claim that 'various books exist complete and unchangeable in my mind—what remains is only to do the actual writing', and it is possible to see why MacDiarmid's canon has been described as a bibliographer's nightmare.

The range of literary projects set out in the letters is matched by MacDiarmid's voracious reading. As in the pre-war years, much of this appetite was fed by literary journalism and there are references to *The English Review*, *Blast*, *The London Mercury*, *Life*, *Everyman*, *The British Weekly*, *The Englishwoman*, *The Month*, *The Tablet*, *The Dublin Leader*, and a good number of European and army journals. There are also on-going references to *The New Age* and its circle, the periodical which Ogilvie had introduced MacDiarmid to during his school years, and which proved to be such a formative influence on MacDiarmid.[5] The earliest of these references occurs in 1911, the year MacDiarmid published his first article in the journal, and it may well have been his success in having this work published which prompted him to contact Ogilvie at that time. Popular writers of the day made up a great deal of MacDiarmid's reading material, probably because these works were more readily available in war-time. John Masefield, Galsworthy, H G Wells, Viola Meynell, George Moore, G K Chesterton, Hilaire Belloc and the Georgian poets are all mentioned. But present too are those writers who are now regarded as 'moderns'—Ezra Pound, Wyndham Lewis, Rebecca West, J M Synge, Joseph Conrad, contemporary French poets and Russian writers.

The cross-currents of MacDiarmid's reading and writing are set out in the glimpses he gives Ogilvie of his 'Suggestion Books'. Wide-ranging in world-lterature as these suggestions are, the Scottish element is never very far away from his plans. Not only does he range through a great list of Scottish historical characters in a way which suggests that even then he was rewriting Scottish history, but there are some surprising combinations. While it is quite within expectations to find Scott, Stevenson, Dunbar, and so on, listed, there is the distinct feeling that only MacDiarmid could discuss 'a copy of Burns I want' side-by-side with plans for a 'Scottish Vortex'.

MacDiarmid began writing poetry in earnest while he was still in the army. His first volume of poems is referred to variously as 'Salonika Poems' and 'A Voice from Macedonia'. By his own admission, MacDiarmid, although he was to write some of the purest poetry of the modern period, also threw off a great deal of dross, and the poems that have survived from this unpublished volume belong to the latter category. MacDiarmid wrote to Ogilvie that these poems were 'the work of three consecutive days, except one or two written earlier and at isolated times. Probably they might be the better for having more time spent on them but that would be rather against the idea of "soldier-verse"—essentially a hasty and spontaneous thing' (28 April 1918). One of these poems, 'Allegiance', was later anthologised in the First Series of *Northern Numbers*:

The ancient chorus of the rich blue flood,
    The mystic sundance of the Middle Seas,
What have you in your heart, Scots Borderman,
    Prithee, that can compare with these?

A brown stream chunners in my heart always.
    I know slim waters that the sun makes dance
With splendid subtlety and suppleness,
    And many a green and golden glance. . . .

These poems show the influence of contemporary Scots verse and are
comparable with the kind of work then being published by leading Scottish
writers, like John Buchan and Neil Munro. Perhaps if MacDiarmid had spent
more of his army service on the Western Front this poetry would have been
quite different and more of a piece with the work of Roderick Watson Kerr, a
schoolfriend of MacDiarmid from Broughton, whose stark war poems earned
him a name as the 'Scottish Sassoon'.

    In the post-war period MacDiarmid began to concentrate more on his poetry
and to send batches of work to Ogilvie. Much of this verse was in sonnet
sequences, characteristically written at great speed and in great quantities. He
wrote, 'A week ago it struck me that it would be an interesting exercise to write
a volume of sonnets. Forthwith I planned a book to consist of . . . 50 in all. I have
so far succeeded in writing . . . the 29 I enclose. I account it a creditable week's
work (24 October 1920). Later, he sent another batch, this time explaining to
Ogilvie that,

> they deal with foreign subjects—Russian, French, Italian, Spanish, Bulgarian—for
> the most part: and are largely unintelligible to those who are not thoroughly familiar
> with the modern literature of these countries. They are highly allusive—but I am
> supplying notes which will be interesting in themselves and thoroughly illuminating.
> I cannot apologise for obscurity of this kind. Some of them derive additional
> 'obscurity' from the fact that they seek to express in concentrated form as it were the
> essence of the paradoxical philosophies of Blake and Nietzsche, etc.
>
> (19 March 1922)

It is difficult to imagine what kind of audience MacDiarmid had in mind for
these sonnets, or what kind of 'ideal reader' would be familiar with such a broad
range of literature, plus the philosophies of Blake and Nietzsche. But the breadth
of the project suggests the sweep of his imagination (and, indeed, the shape of the
later, long poems) as well as his tendency to look, not to England, but to Europe,
for literary ideas. And, of course, his expressed interest in 'paradoxical
philosophies' suggests the direction his aesthetic was taking, he was moving
towards the dialectical play of opposites, and at this point in his development
clearly felt that he could effect higher synthesis within the sonnet form.

    Determined to make his mark in the sonnet, MacDiarmid wrote to Ogilvie,
'My reason for sonneteering instead of writing in other forms is that I want to
write two or three sonnets which will live—which will rank with the great
sonnets of British literature—and once I do write two or three sonnets which a

competent critic assures me fill that bill I shall stop sonneteering' (March 1922?). MacDiarmid was nothing if not ambitious!

But he did begin to branch out and started experimenting with *vers libre*. Perhaps stimulated by Ezra Pound's pre-war articles on modern French verse in *The New Age*,[6] MacDiarmid (in 1919) had been reading 'in the original' an anthology of contemporary French poets, planned to translate their work, and was working on an article entitled, 'the motivation and method of modern French creative art'. The emphasis placed by *vers libristes* on the rhythms of spoken language and their incorporation of colloquial and idiomatic speech into their verse, may have been one of the forces which directed MacDiarmid's attention to the potential of his own vernacular. While in poems like 'Allegiance' MacDiarmid uses Scots vocabulary ('chunners'), the force of individual words is lost because the words operate within a conventional, essentially English, structure. In the *vers libre* poems which MacDiarmid sent to Ogilvie there is no Scots vocabulary, but the language has become more economical and the structure much tighter. This condensing of language, with its accompanying emphasis on rhythm as opposed to standard metre, seems to have acted as a bridge between MacDiarmid's early experiments and his verse in Scots. Certainly, the emphasis placed by the *vers libristes* on exploring the sensory potential of individual words must have played some part in alerting him to the poetic possibilities of the vernacular.

But, as with any question of literary influences, the situation is considerably more complex and in MacDiarmid's case there were influences closer to home which were having their effect.

During his army days, MacDiarmid had been in touch with a number of Scottish writers—John Buchan, John Ferguson, Thomas Scott Cairncross, and others—and had written to Ogilvie about their work. Ogilvie, in turn, urged MacDiarmid to start putting this work together in some form, and the end result was the First Series of *Northern Numbers*, MacDiarmid's earliest editorial venture. The model for this work was *Georgian Poetry*, the English anthologies edited by Edward Marsh. Following Marsh's lead, MacDiarmid brought together the work of mainly well-established poets, a choice which ensured that the volume would receive some attention, and indeed guaranteed its success.

The contributors to the First Series were, for the most part, unknown to each other, and certainly never saw themselves as a distinctive 'group' or movement. But by bringing their work together, MacDiarmid not only put on public display the kind of themes, ideas—and language—which pre-occupied Scottish writers, but also showed that there were new energies at work in Scottish poetry. It was this sense of the new which MacDiarmid carried through to the Second Series, which was to be a much more 'experimental' volume. The inclusion of a large number of women poets (several of them feminists), the amount of space given to 'modern' poems, and the greatly increased representation of verse in the vernacular showed that MacDiarmid was out to set new standards. Indeed, the *Northern Numbers* series demonstrated a new vitality which foreshadowed the literary movement to come.

The verse in Scots which was included in the Second Series—particularly the work of Violet Jacob and Charles Murray—showed that these poets were using the vernacular, not as a nostalgic nod to the past, but as a viable means of expression in the present. Their poems were acts of self-assertion and MacDiarmid could not have been blind to that fact.

MacDiarmid's first poems in Scots were dismissed by him as pieces of 'studio work', which perhaps suggest that his move into Scots was considerably less dramatic than he subsequently painted it. MacDiarmid does not seem to have fully appreciated the significance of his achievement until the work began to receive public acclaim. In the letters to Ogilvie he does not discuss the early stages of his work in Scots, which seems a striking omission for what was subsequently to prove such a major discovery.

The periodical in which he published his early Scots verse, *The Scottish Chapbook*, does get mentioned to Ogilvie but the comments are confined mainly to MacDiarmid asking Ogilvie to help him procure subscribers. The adoption of a pseudonym is discussed. Ogilvie disapproved, but as MacDiarmid explained to him the name had become attached to his work in the vernacular and there was little he could do about it.

It is clear that by the time of the publication of his work in Scots, MacDiarmid had undergone a psychological separation from Ogilvie and had begun to look elsewhere for advice and criticism. This was a gradual break which had been building over a number of years since MacDiarmid's release from the army. As several of the letters suggest, the demands made by MacDiarmid were felt by Ogilvie to be excessive. Ogilvie's retiring temperament must have made it difficult for him to cope with MacDiarmid's kind of intensity, and the sheer amount of work which MacDiarmid was pouring out, made it impossible for anyone to keep apace of him. Ogilvie began to chastise MacDiarmid severely for his unending demands and MacDiarmid's replies to such rebuttals make it clear that he felt betrayed by his mentor:

> Do you think I want money or position or reputation? No. Do you think that it matters to my wife, for instance? I may dedicate my poems to her but do you think that she reads them? And if she did do you think she would understand them or me? No! I need not write. I can dream my books and enjoy them in my head. But I try to write incessantly and cannot help doing so because your commendation of my work is my only desire. If my work gives you no pleasure—if my work does not satisfy you that you saw true away back in those Broughton days—it is wasted, irrespective of anything else. I own no duty, in connection with any power of expression I may have, to anyone, God and man may be, as they like. But for you I will do all that lies within my power, In the light of this, can you understand what it means to me, chaotic among my private tragedies and nourishing myself on this solitary flame, to have you write, 'I have had no time to do more than glance at your sonnets'?
>
> (2 November 1920)

Ogilvie, to his credit, tried to heal the breach, and within a few months MacDiarmid had repaid his support by writing and dedicating to him 'A Moment in Eternity'.

But the strength of the friendship had been broken, and thereafter MacDiarmid virtually ceased to consult Ogilvie about his work. He continued to

From left to right: Edwin Muir, Francis George Scott and his son George, and MacDiarmid. Taken in Montrose in 1924 when Edwin Muir and his wife Willa were living in the High Street. Scott had recently renewed his contact with MacDiarmid and was to help him order the final version of *A Drunk Man looks at the Thistle*.

keep in contact, but the content of the letters of the later years tends more and more to the domestic and the listing by MacDiarmid of his latest publications and achievements.

The fissure which developed between the two men was no doubt widened by MacDiarmid's public and often vitriolic attacks on a number of the stalwarts of Scottish culture. Too often, MacDiarmid seemed to function at his best in confrontation and the more retiring Ogilvie must have found it impossible to defend his actions, particularly when he thought that many of these attacks were unwarranted. MacDiarmid's much publicised attack on the Burns cult was not to Ogilvie's taste and it appears to have been very difficult for the school teacher to accept that this great literary talent he had been so carefully nurturing was a born breaker of icons.

MacDiarmid's increasingly radical political involvement too must have discomfited Ogilvie. While MacDiarmid's move to Communism is not discussed in these letters, his vow to Ogilvie to act on the 'Left Wing' was probably a much more radical stand than Ogilvie was prepared to take, or to support. Nevertheless, MacDiarmid did keep up the contact and when he published his first collections of poems wrote to tell Ogilvie of their reception:

> *Sangschaw* is only a beginning . . . I have another half-ready. I expected S to meet with a mixed reception, and it has. But the people to whose opinion I attach any importance are unanimous. Grierson had doubts as to the validity, practicality and desirability of . . . what I proposed trying to do in my MacDiarmid stuff: but after . . . reading *Sangschaw* he writes as follows:-
>   'I have been reading it with unaffected and great pleasure. You have, I think succeeded in writing Scottish poetry that is quite unaffected by the Burns . . . Sentimental-Kailyard tradition, and which is real poetry, imaginative and moving. One is glad to get in Scots such sincere, imaginative, musical poetry in so fine, and (for later Scotland) so surprising and fresh a strain. . . . I do feel (which I do not often) that you have given me a fresh experience in poetry.'
>
> (September 1925?)

MacDiarmid was obviously delighted that such a distinguished critic of the day as H J C Grierson had recognised the originality of his work, and this in itself was a spur to greater ambitions.

MacDiarmid's major work in Scots, *A Drunk Man Looks at the Thistle*, was already under way when the first two volumes of poetry in Scots were published. The foreword to this work tended to play down the serious vein of the poetry. But, in fact, as the letters reveal, MacDiarmid knew full well that he was committed to creating a masterpiece. Ogilvie had written to congratulate him on the success of *Penny Wheep* and encouraged him to put all his into *A Drunk Man*, and MacDiarmid replied in kind:

> I realise fully the importance of what you urge in regard to the *Drunk Man*. It will either make or finish me so far as Braid Scots work . . . [is] concerned. . . . I've spared no pains and put my uttermost ounce into the business. I'm out to make or break in this matter. . . . It's the thing as a whole that I'm mainly concerned with,

and if, as such, it does not take its . . . place as a masterpiece—sui generis—one of the
biggest things in the range of Scottish Literature, I shall have failed.

(6 August 1926)

After the publication of this major work, MacDiarmid also discussed its
reception with Ogilvie and it is evident that he was deeply disappointed that his
poem had not met with immediate success.

The lack of response to his work in Scotland was one of the factors which
prompted MacDiarmid's move to London. In 1929, accompanied by his family,
MacDiarmid went south to be editor of *Vox*, a periodical dedicated to the new
broadcasting, which was sponsored by Compton MacKenzie. The move to
London was not, as MacDiarmid clearly hoped it would be, the rise of his star in
the literary world. In fact, it proved a disaster. MacDiarmid's forthrightness, his
love of contention and his ability to antagonise, did not stand in his favour.
Unable to compromise to any degree, he soon saw the collapse of his hopes. As
he himself later recognised, this inflexibility in his character affected his private
life and led to the break-up of his marriage. His subsequent divorce, which
received public attention, his excessive drinking, the collapse of several literary
and publishing ventures, all contributed to make the years which followed some
of the most difficult of his whole life. MacDiarmid's roots were in rural Scotland
and his happiest and most productive years were spent as a family man in a small
town. Separated from the kind of stability which that life offered, he was
spiritually lost.

Despite the difficulties of his life in London, there is little in the letters to
Ogilvie about his family situation. Indeed, only rarely does MacDiarmid lay bare
his feelings. Essentially, he was a private man. To Ogilvie he sometimes confided
his troubles, but rarely his torments. These he would refer to obliquely, or cite
them as the reason for his sometimes long lapses into silence. Of the fact that
MacDiarmid had an intense inner life, there can be little doubt. He could never
have produced poetry of such poignancy without that essential element. On
some rare occasions in the letters this intensity slips through, but for the most
part MacDiarmid, despite at times his almost desperate need for Ogilvie's
sympathy and approval, always held the older man at arm's length. The way in
which he signed his letters is a clear indication of this. The formality of 'C M
Grieve' speaks volumes, and only occasionally does he use the more intimate
'Chris' or 'Christopher'. MacDiarmid needed Ogilvie's paternalistic friendship,
but he also recognised that ultimately a poet's battle is fought in the isolation of
his own soul:

> . . . you will know . . . that there is at least one chamber in the heart of every real
> man to which he can admit no other—to which under certain circumstances he dare
> scarcely venture himself—and it is in that secret chamber that the most terrible
> encounters of a life which in any case never set much store by either material or
> spiritual happiness or peace must continue apparently without intermission to be
> fought.

(13 November 1920)

The letters which were written by Ogilvie to MacDiarmid, although few in number, give a sense of the increasing enervation and illness which plagued the teacher in his last years. The letter which closes the correspondence was sent by Ogilvie during his final illness and it is very much the letter of a dying man. That he had lived to see this stormy, uncompromising character create such wondrous poetry must have been the justification of all the faith Ogilvie had placed in MacDiarmid as a young student at Broughton. For his part, MacDiarmid's continued contact with his old teacher speaks of his great loyalty and respect for the man who had helped him through his early struggles.

The correspondence which passed between the two men over a period of almost twenty years is at once the record of an enduring friendship, a barometer of the political and social climate of the day, a history of the origins of the modern Scottish literary movement, and a testament to a young poet's vision. MacDiarmid's literary reputation is secure, it will not rest on his letters alone. But what this correspondence does offer is fresh insight into the movement of this poet's mind. The spontaneity, the wit, the forthrightness, the multiple-mindedness which assaults the reader at every turn can only enhance understanding of a formidable Scotsman and one of the original poets of this century.

Catherine Kerrigan

NOTES

1   J G Sinclair, 'An Old Master' in *Broughton Magazine*, 1960, pp 14–16.

2   *Broughton Magazine*, Christmas 1920, pp 9–13.

3   'George Ogilvie: An Appreciation' in *Hugh MacDiarmid: Early Lyrics*. (Preston: Akros), pp 19–23.

4   *See* Colin Holme's 'The Tredegar Riots of 1911: Anti-Jewish Disturbances in South Wales' in *The Welsh History Review*, December 1982, pp 214–225.

5   For an account of *The New Age* influence see my '*Whaur Extremes Meet: The Poetry of Hugh MacDiarmid, 1920–1934*. (Edinburgh: Mercat Press, 1983).

6   Pound's articles, entitled 'The Approach to Paris', appeared in *The New Age* from September to October 1913. In a letter from Pound to MacDiarmid (now in Edinburgh University Library) written in the 1930s, Pound compares contemporary French poetry to that of the pre-war *vers libristes*.

MacDiarmid, 1927. Photograph by Andrew Paterson, Inverness.

TO VALDA and MICHAEL GRIEVE

PART ONE

1911–1919

Biographical Summary

Hugh MacDiarmid was born on 11 August 1892 at Arkinholm Terrace in Langholm, a small town close to the border of Scotland and England. He was the youngest son of the town's postman and grew up in a family environment of Presbyterianism and Trade Unionism. When he reached school age MacDiarmid was sent to Langholm Infant School, transferring from there in 1899 to Langholm Academy. In 1908 he went to Edinburgh to enroll at Broughton Junior Student Centre and there had his first contact with Ogilvie.

MacDiarmid left Broughton in 1911 without completing his teacher training. His father died on 3 February of that year and there then followed a period of great disquiet in the young MacDiarmid's life as he tried to contend with the loss of his father and the need to begin to make his way in the world in his own independent terms. Ogilvie helped him to get a job as junior reporter on the *Edinburgh Evening Dispatch*, but after a few months he left his job, probably because of a dispute with an editor (*see* letter 9 November 1921). He moved thereafter to South Wales to work once again as a journalist. At the time MacDiarmid was nineteen years old.

c/o J W Storey
55 Harcourt Street,
Ebbw Vale, Monmouthshire,
South Wales.[1]

[August 1911?]
Today. (Friday, I think, or Saturday).

Dear Mr Ogilvy, [*sic*]

It's one in the morning and I've just transcribed my last sheaf of notes.

I don't know why I feel that I must write to you now or never. I have tried to do it a dozen times.

I will never return to Edinburgh—to stay at all events. Probably I'll never see you again, but I feel that you understand better than anybody else I know—that you will be glad to know that it is all right, that I have at last emerged from chaos—from the hurricane of mental and moral anarchy which has tossed me hither-and-thither these last twelve months.

I am in a good position, earning good money, working fifteen or sixteen hours a day.

And I look back to you as I look back to my dead father, to my mother,[2] and one or two others.

Enclose[d] you will find a cutting—which perhaps may interest Mr Ross more than you.[3] I should be glad if you would return it, as it is the only copy I possess.

Yours sincerely,

Christopher Grieve.

P.S.   Please let us keep up a correspondence.

NOTES

1   Ebbw Vale, in the heart of the South Wales coalfield was, before 1914, the largest coal-exporting district in the world. It later became (and still is) the heart of the Welsh strength in the Labour Party. During the time MacDiarmid was in Wales, the miners had begun to organise and tensions in the area were running high. As the letter which follows indicates, MacDiarmid was on the spot when civil strife erupted.
2   James Grieve (1864–1911) and Elizabeth Grieve (neé Graham) (1866–1934?).
3   Peter Ross was Maths Master at Broughton and also gave classes in astronomy. The cutting was probably a copy of 'The Young Astrology' which had been published in *The New Age* (20 July 1911, p 274).

55 Harcourt Street,
Ebbw Vale,
Mon, S Wales.

24 October 1911

Dear Mr Ogilvie,

Forging ahead aye! I have already been instrumental in forming four new branches of the ILP[1] down here. In Tredegar a policeman took my name and address on the grounds that it was illegal to speak off the top of a soap-box.

I asked him if a match-box was within the meaning of the act and he put something else down in his note-book: what I do not know.

However, as a branch of 25 members was the outcome, I can afford to be generous.

Did you see any account of the recent pogroms in Bargoed, Tredegar, Rhymney, Ebbw Vale and Cum?[2] They gave me my first taste of war corresponding: and I narrowly escaped being bludgeoned more than once. I heard the Riot Act[3] read thrice in one night (in different towns, of course) and saw seventeen baton charges. My attack on the police, for their conduct during these riots, sent up the sales of the paper considerably.[4] I did not get to bed for four consecutive nights and was the only reporter present at the meeting of the rioters—the riots were almost as admirably directed as the present Chinese revolution[5]—held at Nantybuc at midnight and my editor thought fit to warn me that in all probability I would be arrested for aiding and abetting.

I have since investigated the matter thoroughly; and the Urban District Councils are agog at the outcome, which reveals an almost incredibly inhuman system of rack-renting and blood-sucking on the part of the Jews in the district.

Several police cases are already filed: I will post you cuttings of my revelations shortly.

I am also busy every minute I can spare in doing up the Broughton business—in anonymous terms, of course—after the style of these 'Tales for Men Only' that have been appearing in The New Age[6] to which my efforts will also be directed as soon as I complete and polish—say in a fortnight or three weeks.

When you write that Mr Ross did not seem to understand my article, do you mean that he could not understand such an article coming from me: or do you mean it literally, because, if so, I might post him a little scientific dictionary in memory of old times.

I will send you cuttings of all original stuff from my pen-nib and ink bottle.

I have piles of stuff in chaos; and if I had not such an impossible district to cover, could sort some of it out and dress it up. But my district includes several large mining towns—with all sorts of sectional strikes, inquests, colliery accidents and Federation meetings.

It's like living on the top of a volcano down here. You never know what's going to happen next. I have had three triple murders this last fornight: and have two strikes in hand now. Tomorrow there is County Court in Tredegar—over 400 cases filed, nearly all connected with mining compensation etc.

I am kept pretty well informed of Broughton affairs—(Do not press the point. Open confession may be good for the soul: but there are other things to consider) but would like to have a syllabus of this winter's lit: and copies of the magazine.

The astrological article was—I think I did not mention it before—only one of a forthcoming series. I have several important new and absolutely original propositions to enunciate: and have had quite a long and interesting correspondence with Camille Flammarion[7] and Prof A W Bickerton (of Yale Observatory):[8] more of that anon.

I wish I could find time to formulate them soon: also I want to publish a little booklet on Theology.[9]

I wish some device could be patented whereby my flying thoughts could be photographed: that might give me a chance to express my present mental stage with some adequacy.

As to physique, I am constantly crossing mountains (by unutterably rocky tracks) and the wind and rain and constant outdoor work is doing good.

My hair is as outré as ever.

Hoping to hear from you soon.

Yours etc.

C M Grieve.

P.S.   There must be a hiatus somewhere in my humanitarianism. A society for the prevention of cruelty to friends should be formed and I should be sentenced to death for inflicting such an atrociously long and aimless letter in such execrable caligraphy, on an unfortunate friend.

Do tell me about your Canadian trip and give my kindest respects to Mrs Ogilvie.

C.M.G.

26 October 1911

[Sketch of a clock with hands pointing to 1.25]

NOTES

1 The Independent Labour Party, founded in 1893 through the merging of several socialist societies under the leadership of Keir Hardie (1856–1915).

2 There were civil riots in these towns in South Wales at various times in 1911. Events have not yet been adequately chronicled, so it is difficult to give a complete picture, but from September 1910 on there was growing agitation in the area over working-class conditions. The miners had struck for a minimum working wage and for improvements in the safety conditions at the collieries. Their demonstrations were met with drastic measures on the part of the police force and, on other occasions, by the military. The situation was compounded by the fact that the railway strike had artificially inflated the price of goods in the shops and had also led to shortages of food supplies. This, coupled with awful housing conditions and generally poor standards of living, led to spontaneous riots in which even very respectable members of the community were involved. The riots in Tredegar had also an anti-Jewish element. Several Jewish families there were large property owners and shopkeepers. The combination of the high rents and the inflated cost of goods made these families the focus of the attacks. (*See* Colin Holme's 'The Tredegar Riots of 1911: Anti-Jewish Disturbances in South Wales' in *The Welsh History Review*, December 1982, pp 214–25).

3 The Riot Act provided that if assemblies of twelve or more persons failed to disperse after the reading by an official of a proclamation ordering them to do so, they would be guilty of a felony.

4 MacDiarmid worked for the *Monmouthshire Labour News* which was set up in 1907 by the Miners Federation. There are no copies of this newspaper in the National Library of Wales, the British Library, the Glamorgan Archives or the Gwent Record Office at Cwmbran and it therefore seems unlikely that it survived.

5 The Chinese People's Revolution which led in 1912 to the abdication of the Emperor and the subsequent establishing of the Chinese Republic.

6 These were a series of articles which appeared in *The New Age* from August 1911 to November 1912. Written mainly by Alfred Richard Orage, using the pseudonym R H Congreve, they purported to explore the effects of female emancipation on traditional relationships. MacDiarmid's proposed article never materialised.

7 Camille Flammarion (1842–1925), French astronomer and populariser of the subject.

8 Alexander William Bickerton (1842–1929), Professor of Physics and Chemistry at Canterbury College, University of New Zealand. He too was a populariser of astronomy and had put forward a controversial theory of cosmic construction in his *The Birth of Worlds and Systems* (1911).

9 There is no trace of this work.

There is a gap of over four years in the correspondence at this point. In the intervening years MacDiarmid had returned from Wales to Langholm where he lived with his mother before taking up another job as a reporter on the *Clydebank and Renfrew Press*. In that same year, 1912, he moved yet again, this time to Cupar in Angus where he worked for three associated newspapers and where he met the girl who was to be his first wife, Margaret Skinner. In 1913 he moved to Forfar and worked on the *Forfar Review* until, in 1915, he enlisted. After a period of training at Aldershot he went with the Royal Army Medical Corps to Salonika where he was to serve in the 42nd General Hospital.

By the time MacDiarmid arrived in Greece in August 1916 the evacuation of Gallipoli had been completed and the action of the war now began to be concentrated on the Western Front. Verdun and the Battle of the Somme were in progress and the Central Powers had begun their attack on Serbia. Greece had declared neutrality, so that the Allied presence there was a very uneasy one and remained so until King Constantine was deposed and Venizelos was elected Premier.

At home, the armed insurrection in Ireland which would be known as the Easter Rising had taken place from 24 to 29 April. The Irish Republican Brotherhood and the Citizen Army under the leadership of Patrick Pearse and James Connolly took up central positions in Dublin on Easter Monday 1916 and Pearse subsequently proclaimed the establishment of the Irish Republic. After a week of fighting, the insurgents surrendered unconditionally and fifteen of the leaders, including Pearse and Connolly, were executed.

In Scotland there were many who were sympathetic to the bid for Irish independence and the cause had received much publicity through James Connolly who was Irish Correspondent for the radical socialist journal, *Forward*. During the war, the political situation in Scotland was far from stable. Clydeside, with its attendant coal and steel industries, had become one of the main centres of shipbuilding and munitions. But the control of heavy industry by the war government became a focal point of disturbance. In 1915 engineers had struck over a wage claim and were denounced as traitors. The reaction of the workers was increased Trade Union support and the formation of the Clyde Workers Committee, a group which opposed the Munitions of War Act and the kind of militarism which that Act forced upon workers. The spread of the influence of this committee to centres of industry outside of Scotland was becoming a source of government anxiety when, in 1916, Lloyd George became Prime Minister. His government responded to the situation by suppressing left-wing journals and imprisoning those associated with them. The movement, however, survived and grew in strength towards the end of the war, becoming increasingly radical and even, at one point, revolutionary.

In Russia the mutiny at the Petrograd garrison on 10 March 1917 signalled the beginning of the Russian Revolution. Nicholas II abdicated and the Bolshevik-dominated Petrograd-Soviet (Council of Workers and Soldiers' Deputies) pledged itself to continue the war against the Central Powers until an Allied victory was achieved. However, fearing a counter-revolution from the officer corps, the Soviet issued 'Order No. 1', thus depriving officers of any authority. The result was the assassination of a large percentage of the commanding officers and the complete breakdown of the Russian army, the effect of which was not only the weakening of the Allied Forces, but widespread fears that British and French troops might follow the Russian lead.

The long letter which follows refers to events at home and abroad and was written by MacDiarmid some two weeks after he arrived in Greece. Part of this letter was edited and published by Ogilvie in the *Broughton Magazine* (Christmas 1917, pp 20–1) and formed one of a series from former pupils on active service which was entitled, 'Letters from the Front'.

Somewhere in Macedonia[1]

20 August 1916

Dear Mr Ogilvie,

The Sergeant-Caterer of the Officers' Mess (that's my new post in our little military world here) has to go 'on deck' at dinner—dinner commencing at 7.30p.m. and running to some five courses—freshly-shaven, boots and buttons mirror-bright, properly dressed with belt and all. He does nothing, of course, save supervision. A spot of tarnish on a knife or fork—lack-lustre of a wine-glass—uneven flaming of one of the hanging lamps—slackness on the part of the waiters—slow, slovenly, or uneven dishing-up on the part of the cooks—what an eye one develops for detail on such a job! Between the Mess-Marquée, and the Mess cook-house, is a strip of open hillside over which the waiters run backwards and forwards in the moony Macedonian night. Brightly the beams fall on platefuls of white vegetable soup, patum peperium entrées, portions of cottage pie enlivened with rice-stuffed peppers, liberal helpings of rice and raisins, coffee pots – – – and later when the Mess has come to the walnuts and almonds and the wine-steward is busy supplying Vinc Blanc, Vin Russe, or Vin Muscat de Samos (my favourite wine, recalling with every sip the wonderful tribute of a poem of Mr Sturge Moore's[2] and unreservedly endorsing every adjective therein), the Sergeant-Caterer and his staff dine too. (What an awful war, to be sure!)

Then down the hill a bit to the Sergeant's Mess Marquée to see if there are any letters—to play a hand at solo-whist at a penny a corner or, out of purest spite perhaps, or because the courses of the dinner ran too like true love or simply from nostalgia talk like a Bernard Shaw preface, irritatingly over their heads, with bewildering rapidity and not very obvious consequence, and yet with sufficient point and wit to make them endure me. And then up the hill again to my store here where amid stacks of Nestlé's Milk, tinned jams and cakes, sacks of potatoes, bags of flour and oatmeal, tins of tapioca and rice and café-au-lait and cocoanut and cornflour, bottles of wine and whisky and A1 relish I have my bed and my desk and an excellent lamp and a book or two—Gardiner's *Prophets, Priests and Kings*,[3] Birrell's *Selected Essays*,[4] R L's *Familiar Studies of Men and Books*, assorted copies of the *Nation, Spectator* and *New Witness*.[5]

And I read an hour or two. Perhaps do a little scribbling. Another paragraph or two, or merely a note of a line of thought, for my 'Scots Church Essays', or 'Scots Art Essays', thus (extracted from my notebook at random)

8.   The Calibre of Modern Scottish Priests. (Contrast with America where, vide Monsignor Benson,[6] 'Catholicism is the only living religion').

9.   Neo-Catholicism's debt to Sir Walter Scott. (This completed—based on Newman's and Borrow's acknowledgements).[7]

10. The Indisserverable Association. (i.e. of Catholicism in Scotland—like bells of Ys.[8] Placenames, social functions, sacraments, etc. etc. This also completed).

The first series of these 'studies' runs to 50.[9] So does the second, embracing

1. The Religion of Wallace[10] and Bruce[11] (and all great figures of Scottish history— the religion which makes the true atmosphere of Scottish tradition. Who shall put Peden[12] beside Bonnie Prince Charlie,[13] Jenny Geddes[14] beside Queen Margaret?[15] etc).

11. On Scottish Religious and Moral Influences overseas.

17. Files of Futility. (Scots Church papers—a distinctionless infinitude of number).

18. Scots Catholic Soldiery.

21. Our Loss of Negative Capability.[16]

40. John Knox[17] and Mrs "General" Drummond:[18] an Imaginary Interview. Completed. Not bad, I think, but deriving, of course, from R.L.S. on "Knox's Relations with women".[19]

etc. etc.

Or is it Art?
I have my 'The Scottish Vortex' (as per system exemplified in *Blast*),[20] 'Caricature in Scotland—and lost opportunities', 'A Copy of Burns I want', (suggestions to illustrators on a personal visualization of the national pictures evoked in the poem), 'Scottish colour-thought' (a study of the aesthetic condition of Scottish nationality in the last three centuries) and 'The Alienation of Our Artistic Ability' (the factors which prevent the formation of a 'national' school and drive our artists to other lands and to foreign portrayal).

But tonight I have not added a note or thought of a new topic. Tonight when dinner [was] over I went down to the Sergeants' Mess [where] your letter was lying for me. I opened it and a bottle of beer and sat down to read—and when I had finished the forgotten beer had gone hopelessly flat. And beer, not bad beer but not 'the good brown ale' by a long chalk, being sourer and thinner, is 80 leptae (eightpence) a kilo-bottle in this Paradise of War-Profiteers. But I did not grudge the eightpence nor did I have another bottle, but bought instead some sweets, remembering what Huxley says somewhere concerning the energising qualities of sugar, and knowing that I should require all my energy.

Your letter was not only in itself a joy: but because of myself an unspeakable relief. 'Twere hopeless to try to convey the state of mind it has occasioned to me—the mingling of memories, desires, regrets, hopes, aye and still fears.

Fears—for I shall never read a letter of yours or think a thought of you without a sense of shame and a terrible unrest until I have something worthwhile [to] dedicate to you. But enough of that! You know and I know. And I have not done it yet.

And mention of that makes me think painfully of another debt I owe, to a dream unredeemed in his life but vital to me in the very fibre of my being, and unthinkable to go unpaid. You mention Nisbet.[21] What Nisbet was to me (although for long before his death we had not met nor corresponded) I cannot define—infinitely more than a brother, a very spiritual familiar—one of the many contrasting personalities in me was essentially Nisbet, thinking in me with his brain, working in me with his splendid sensuous vitality, reflecting upon the other personalities, part and parcel of the debating society which is my mental life. He must not go undedicate—I have the very poem (for poem it must be without saying). It trembles on my tongue—at times in semi-sleep I can read it in the volumes of my subconsciousness as from a printed page—perfect, adequate. But I have not yet contrived to write it. Must I forever plan what I shall never execute? I am tortured worse than any Tantalus. (These personalities of mine stultify each other—I have meant what I have written—Nisbet was terribly my friend—but yet, close on the above, the Humorous Bit must interject, 'Those classical allusions again!' You must stick to the times, you know. Leave Tantalus alone, and confess rather that you are a dead Barber's Cat, becalmed and suffering from a stricture of the urethra.)[22]

The sweets have justified Huxley. My mental machinery is running at top-gear. It is only 9.30 p.m. My lamp I had filled an hour or so ago. Certain 'Salonika Nightingales' (the ubiquitous and racous [sic] donkeys) are making the night hideous but I am used to them, and to the singing all evening long of irrepressible allied troops not far away. Otherwise there is no noise. Nor is there anybody about. I am unlikely to be disturbed again tonight. And you say that you would give much to know in some detail my psychological history since you last saw me; I wish I could comply. How often I have tried—modelling on Amiel's *Journal*,[2] or in novel form, or in a set of essays, or somehow, anyhow. But I have not managed it so far. As you say of the war, so far I am too close to it all. If I could make a peace between my contending spirits—cease to think new thoughts, dream new dreams, live so unceasingly and at such a rate (for I can think out novels and plays in odd half-hours, visualize every detail, see them published and played, anticipate their criticisms in *The Times*, *The British Weekly* and *The New Age* simultaneously, write prefaces to new editions, sum up carefully on the business side, grant interviews and talk at great length and with indescribable sense and spirit—and as promptly forget all about them: although they all stick in my consciousness and my thoughts are thus forever like a man moving through the ever-increasing and various confusion of an enormous higgledy-piggledy lumber-room)—if, as I was saying before I put out that leafy branch, I could get a sufficient breathing space, then I think I could take stock and write myself forever out of the tangle. That done, I could obtain that variety which is the spice of life, by getting into another and quite different but no less complex tangle.

But I cannot get that breathing space. Nor can I hit on any super-shorthand to keep pace with my continuing mental 'spate' and make up back-time. The outlines are capable of being jotted down very barely perhaps

1.   South Wales—working for Miners' Federation[24]—delightfully immersed in labour movement, until perception into spiritual sides of question got beyond ILP stage—then found myself in an atmosphere suddenly transfused with hostility—youth and natural tactlessness accentuated difficulty—would I had been born jesuitical—as it was shipwrecked on hidden rocks of implacable liberalism and non-conformity suddenly in bright seas of labourist activity. Contrived to have published in sacro-sanct columns extremist articles galling to diplomatists like Tom Richards, MP,[25] and other Miners' Leaders on editorial committee. Was horribly unrepentant and truculent withal. Openly construed their statesmanship as a species of hypocrisy attributable to the partial development of too generous ideals in unsuitable natures. Re-organisation of paper afforded convenient opportunity of dispensing with my services.

2.   Back home again to Langholm. Living practically, as Bernard Shaw did, off my widowed mother. Reading inordinately (a fault persisted in to such an extent at too tender an age as to be largely responsible for my present predicament), and spasmodically writing enough to bring in an average of say £1 a week, of which I smoked and purchased papers to the extent of, say, 25%. Philandered extensively during this period. Intimate passages with three young ladies, all English, revived in me our racial antipathy to the English, which, recurring lately, has caused me to write quite a body (some thirty poems in all) of Anti-English verse,[26] not dissimilar to certain products of Irish revival.[27] More important is the way in which my attention for the first time was turned to Scottish Nationalism and national problems[28]—my continuing absorption in which is patent in the beginning of this document. Later fell seriously in love with a Scotch girl, a school teacher. Began to work hard, buoyed up with new dreams of honour, visions of a "home of my own", etc. (You can easily complete the picture—ambition stirred, all better instincts at work, my whole being suffused with a new spirit.)

3.   As a consequence of this 'affaire', found work in Clydebank and Renfrew district.[29] A cushie job, but poorly paid. Lived a strenuous life there for some five months—little time for reading or original writing, all reporting. Did nothing discreditable during this period (albeit the ILP again reclaimed me, and poor Maxton[30] and MacLean[31] and I were great friend and co-propagandists) except perhaps for a little interlude with a Dunoon

girl, which clashed nastily with the other affaire owing to a rank inadvertance. But matters adjusted themselves nicely and my brother[32] securing for me an option on a job in Cupar,[33] at a very much higher wage, this fitted in nicely with my unusually-sustained dream of getting into a fairly well-to-do position and marrying and settling down.

4.   In Cupar as assistant-editor of the Innes papers—the *Fife Herald, St. Andrews' Citizen,* and *Fife Coast Chronicle.* Unfortunately in the eyes of my well-wishing relatives Cupar happens to be a boozy little hole and my too-fellow pressmen, representatives respectively of the *Dundee Courier* and the *Dundee Advertiser* were born boon-fellows both. I had heaps of work—holding the correspondencies for the *Glasgow Herald, Glasgow Evening Times, Scotsman, Edinr. Evening Dispatch,* Press Assocn. and Central Newsagency in addition to reporting in extenso for my own three papers. I enjoyed Cupar immensely—worked harder than I should have believed it possible for me to do and simultaneously drank like a fish, acquiring in time the art, of which Dallas[34] of the *Glasgow Herald*—(and perhaps the finest journalist in Scotland today)—is the best exponent, of accurately transcribing and telephonically transmitting while wildly intoxicated reports from the shorthand of brother-journalists who, collapsing under the strain of work and wine, had passed into hopeless conditions which left it up to the unbowled-over one of the party to see that their papers were not 'let down'.

Unfortunately or fortunately, I did not get on well with one of the bosses. We were mutually incompatible. A rupture beyond repair at last sent me to a new sphere in Forfar.[35]

5.   Forfar is the boosiest place on Earth. And again the men with whom I was associated were jolly good fellows. Our libations were limitless. So far did this go, in fact, (although my work never suffered—that is to say my work in the limited sense excluding what I am pleased to consider my life-work) that a sudden access of unaccountable good sense made me take a house, four miles in the country by Glamis Castle way, and invite my mother to keep house for me. The result was eminently satisfactory. I had an easy and well-paid job: my mother had claims upon my time which kept me out of 'company' in my spare time, and I had peace to write. And write I had begun to do in very earnest: but by this time, just when my literary projects were at last emerging out of the tangle and bit by bit getting *actually and satisfactorily*—that is, fairly satisfactorily—written, it was becoming impossible for a young man physically fit to remain in 'civvies'. Besides, I was always susceptible to fits of wanderlust—and I had been a Territorial[36] and loved camping out—and Nisbet's death finally settled matters. (NB—No 'patriotism', no 'fight for civilisation'!)

6.   I joined the Army in July 1915. Within six months of joining I had risen

from a recruit to be Acting Quarter-Master-Sergeant of a Company 1000 strong. I had acquired not only discipline, a certain mastery of and confidence in myself, and a command of men but a sense of responsibility, a certain business ability, and the habit of being trusted and trustworthy. Needless to say in a Sergeants' Mess sobriety is not strictly insisted upon. I drank as heavily as I possibly could without bad effect to my work and position—and it is wonderful how very heavily that is. In full rig-out with sling-sword belt, and polished crowns, and knee-breeches and tan boots, I was 'some nut' too, and English girls are notoriously 'free', especially since the war began—and I prosecuted feminist studies of the nature I have already mentioned to a great extent. But I got no black mark on my papers, and I never failed my CO or Sergeant-Major in the slightest respect.

7.   In July last I was sent to Aldershot: lost (by the curious custom) my acting rank of QMS; in a week or two came through in orders with the substantive (permanent) rank of Sergeant; and was detailed to proceed with this unit, which we did early in August.

So there you are. That's a bald outline. Of my progress through the pit of Atheism to Roman Catholicism (adherent not member of the Church of Rome—I doubt my faiths and doubt my doubts of my faiths too subtly to take the final step but at this house by the wayside am content meanwhile) I have said nothing—but the course is familiar. And similar to it is that other from Labourism through Anarchy to a form of Toryism. And not new either is the general lover whom multiplying loves but confirm in bachelordom. Nor of my ceaseless reading, wide as the world of books, in every conceivable subject—or my interests in activities ranging from gardening to bacteriology and from fox-hunting to scientific indexing—I have planned books and articles on a thousand and one topics (and written in rough draft a score or so—God only knows if they will ever come to more). My mental methods are only too well illustrated by the extracts from my notebook in the beginning of this letter. But I still hope to be allowed to fulfil a few of my intellectual engagements.

I shall come back and start a new Neo-Catholic movement. I shall enter heart and body and soul into a new Scots Nationalist propaganda. I shall—I may.

And now I must make an end. I have no time left for the nonce to animadvert on things Salonikan—to tell you of the life here where all the armies and navies of the world seem to have met—where Russian, Frenchman, Italian, Greek pro-ally revolutionary, Serb and Britisher meet and make friends in Café and Canteen and a curious polyglottery is the current medium of expression—of mosquitoes and rats and locusts and crickets—of heat-strokes at noon and frost-bite at night—of malaria[37] (which I have had badly but have well recovered from, despite occasional agues) and enteric and dysentery—of 'swazi phantazeers' (or little money-makings) in the Sergeants' Mess— of Venizelos[38] and Eshad Pashi[39] and the wonders of Eastern sunsets, and the beauty of villages that clamber on hill-tops—and of a Greece that is not Helas, and yet has new and quite satisfactory Helens (in extenuation I must not forget to tell you that the young lady teacher of stage 2 broke off our engagement last New Year)—but these and other things will keep for again.

Probably I am more in touch even than you are with the Broughtonians contemporary with me.

A curious study in itself would be that of the relations between Miss Murray[40] and I. Months elapse during which we hear nothing of each other. Then suddenly from one or other of us comes a postcard or letter, with never a sense of interval and never a change of tone. We meet haphazardly at long intervals— here or there—Edinburgh or Aberdeenshire or London. And from her I derive my news. I knew of Sutherland and Tommy Clow and Mr Ross:[41] and once in a while of Westwood and T G P Walker and Templeton and Simpson.[42]

From my mother I had just heard before I got your letter of the honour awarded to Dr Drummond's son,[43] and in a sudden access of grateful recollection, have written to congratulate the good doctor.

I am sorry to hear of Mr Watson's[44] recurring illness.

And wish inarticulately I could pop in to Broughton again and sit through a lesson with you: and canvass for contributions to the Magazine[45] in the corridor afterwards: and help to revive the 'Lit':[46] and infuse my tame successors with some new Macedonian madness.

But it is no new thing to wish one had one's life to live over again.

You do not mention any literary activity on your own part: nor tell me how time is dealing with yourself in the respect of health.

To end, may this long letter find you in the best of health and spirits,

with many thanks,

Your[s] Affectionately

C M Grieve

NOTES

1 The 42nd General Hospital was located on the outskirts of Salonika towards Kalamaria in L'Orphenilat Grec.

2 Thomas Sturge Moore (1870–1944), English poet and artist, brother of G E Moore the philosopher. The poem referred to is probably Moore's 'The Vinedresser' (1899).

3 Alfred George Gardiner (also wrote under the pseudonym, 'Alpha of the Plough') (1865–1946). English journalist, editor and writer. *Prophets, Priests and Kings* (1908).

4 Augustine Birrell (1850–1933): politician and writer, he was Liberal MP for West Fife (1889–90) and Irish Secretary (1907–16) from which post he resigned after the Sinn Fein rebellion. *Selected Essays: 1884–1907* (1909).

5 Robert Louis Stevenson (1850–94), *Familiar Studies of Men and Books* (1882). *The Nation*, a weekly literary periodical published in London from 1907–21, after which it combined with *The Athenaeum* to form *The Nation and Athenaeum*. *The Spectator*, then, as now, a weekly journal of news, politics and literature. *The New Witness*, a weekly review of topical affairs which included some literature, published in London from 1912–23 and edited by G K Chesterton.

6 Robert Hugh Benson (1871–1914). Son of Edward White Benson, Archbishop of Canterbury, he was ordained in the Anglican Church, but in 1903 converted to Catholicism. He wrote a number of historical and modern novels, all with a Roman Catholic emphasis: *The Sentimentalists* (1906), *The Queen's Tragedy* (1906), *Come Rack! Come Rope!* (1912).

7 Scott's imaginative sympathy for the Middle Ages made him a particularly appealing writer to Catholic converts. In *Apologia pro Vita sua* (1864), Newman had praised Scott for his depiction of the Middle Ages and felt that he offered an alternative vision to that of industrial society. George Borrow, on the other hand, denounced Scott (in his appendix to *Romany Rye* (1857)) as the man who had brought back Popery.

8 A reference to the legend of the submerged city found in Celtic folklore. In these stories the city is invariably lost at the height of its power through some act of pride. Claims to have seen the palaces and towers are a recurrent element of the stories, all of which make reference to the fertility and beauty of the city under the sea and of the continuity of life there. (*See* John Rhys's *Celtic Folklore*, II, pp 415–19). MacDiarmid is using the reference as a metaphor for the influence of past Catholicism on Scottish culture. *See* his use of the image in 'From *Water of Life*' (*C.P.* II, pp 1213–15).

9 These 'studies' were never published under any of the titles indicated, but much of the material was probably absorbed into various articles MacDiarmid was to publish after his army service when, in campaigning for a Scottish literary revival, he was constantly to refer back to the cultural richness of pre-Reformation days.

10 Sir William Wallace (*c.* 1274–1305). Champion of Scottish independence, he defeated Edward I's army at the battle of Stirling Bridge in 1297 and drove the English army out of Scotland. Subsequently elected governor of Scotland, he was defeated in battle at Falkirk in 1298 and taken to London where he was hanged, drawn and quartered.

11 Robert I (*c.* 1274–1329). He had joined the Scottish revolt under Wallace and after Wallace's death rose against Edward. In 1306 he claimed the Scottish throne and was crowned king at Scone. His greatest battle was fought at Bannockburn in 1314, where the English under Edward II with 1,000,000 men were routed by the Scottish army which was only 30,000 strong. The great hero of the Scottish War of Independence, Bruce's position as King of Scots was secured with the Treaty of Northampton (1328) which recognised Scotland's sovereignty. He died of leprosy at Cardross Castle on the Firth of Clyde and his body was interred in Dunfermline Abbey.

12 Alexander Peden (*c.*1626–86), Scottish covenanting preacher. Ordained in 1660 he was ejected from the ministry for failure to have his appointment collated by the bishop. He subsequently wandered throughout the country preaching mainly to the peasantry, many of whom regarded him as a prophet.

13 Charles Edward Stewart (1720–88), son of James II, he became the centre of Jacobite hopes when in 1745 he landed in Scotland and raised an army which defeated the English at the Battle of Prestonpans. The Scottish army then advanced as far as Derby, but later retreated to Culloden where the English army under the leadership of the Duke of Cumberland slaughtered the Scottish forces, a defeat which sounded

the destruction of the clan system and the Jacobite Rising. A great romantic hero. 'The Young Pretender', is the subject of many songs and stories. He escaped from Scotland and lived in exile in France and Italy. He died in Italy and is buried in the Vatican.

14 Jenny Geddes, a Scottish vegetable-seller who is reputed to have started a riot in St Giles Cathedral in Edinburgh on Sunday, 23 July 1637, when Laud's prayer book was introduced. According to popular legend she threw a stool at the Bishop shouting, 'Thou false thief, dost thou say mass at my lug?'

15 Saint Margaret (c.1045–93), a Saxon princess, b. Hungary, she married the Scottish king, Malcolm Canmore, and with him did a great deal to introduce reforms in Scotland. She assimilated the old Celtic Church to the rest of Christendom and re-founded Iona. She built Dunfermline Abbey and many hospices and was renowned for her personal ministerings to the poor. Canonised in 1251, there are many legends and place names which relate to her.

16 Keats's term for the poet's ability to negate or lose himself in an imaginative identification with something larger than himself.

17 John Knox (c.1513–72), the leader of the Scottish Reformation, he originally took Catholic orders until he caught the zeal of the Lutheran Reformation. Forced to flee to Geneva, he was to be greatly influenced by Calvin. After reformers committed themselves to religious revolution by the *First Covenant* (1557, Knox returned and was instrumental in establishing Protestantism as the religion of Scotland. His reputation as an anti-feminist stems from his *First Blast of the Trumpet against the Monstrous Regiment of Women* (1558), a work which attacked the political power of the Catholic Mary of Guise and which later brought him into conflict with her daughter, Mary Queen of Scots.

18 Mrs Flora Drummond, a Scottish suffragette who was a telegraphist from Arran. One of the first members of the Women's Social and Political Union which was inaugurated in 1903 by Christabel and Emmeline Pankhurst as a woman's branch of the ILP, she earned the title of 'General', not only for her organisational ability and her audacious harassment of parliamentarians in the years before the franchise, but also because she dressed in a military style and led suffragette protests riding on a horse.

19 In Stevenson's *Familiar Studies*. Stevenson presents Knox as much more sympathetic to women than his reputation would suggest.

20 *Blast*, the periodical of the Vorticist school, co-edited by Wyndham Lewis and Ezra Pound. Vorticism adopted an extremist attitude in the typographically revolutionary pages of *Blast* by listing the orthodoxies of British culture which were to be 'blasted'. The Vortex (like the natural phenomenon which the name suggests) was to function as a movement 'from which, and through which, and into which ideas are constantly rushing' (*Blast*, 1914). The periodical attacked the work of Rupert Brooke (who had recently died in the war) and was subsequently denounced. There were only two issues, 20 June 1914 and July 1915.

21 John Bogue Nisbet, a fellow Broughtonian and particular friend. MacDiarmid recalled that he and Nisbet 'used to go cycling and camping in Berwickshire and elsewhere in the Borders, and carried with us little volumes of translations from contemporary French, German and Belgium poets' ('Dr Grieve's Address', *Broughton Magazine*, 1955, p 46). One of MacDiarmid's earliest literary efforts had Nisbet as the title character, *Nisbet: An Interlude in Post-War Glasgow* (serialised in two parts in *The Scottish Chapbook*, August 1922, pp 15–19, September 1922, pp 46–50). MacDiarmid saw Nisbet as a fellow poet who would have established a great reputation for himself had he not been killed in action at the Battle of Loos in 1915.

22 Quotation unidentified.

23 Henri Frédéric Amiel (1821-81), Swiss writer and Professor at Geneva University who is known for his posthumously published *Journal Intime* (1883), a work which explores the author's creative impotence and his inability to find purpose in existence. *See* MacDiarmid's poem 'Amiel' , *C.P.* II, pp 1218-19 and letter March 1922?.

24 The Miners' Federation was set up in 1889, initially to fight for a minimum wage rate. By 1911 the organisation was nationwide and wielded the largest body of votes in the Trades Union Congress. The Federation had also by that time more than fifteen mining representatives in Parliament who were beginning to make their power felt. Most of the founders of the Federation were Methodists and supported peaceful means of pursuing their ends but after the bitter experience of Tonypandy and the brutal police handling of other civil riots in South Wales, the organisation became increasingly militant. (*See* R Page Arnot's *The Miners: Years of Struggle*). The Miners' Federation is now the National Union of Mineworkers.

25 Thomas Richards (1859-1931), Liberal MP elected in 1906. Initially the policies of the Liberal majority were supported by those representing the miners and the other industrial workers. But in 1909 the Miners Federation of Great Britain officially affiliated with the Labour Party and from then on there was an increasing divergence of interests between Liberal and Labour supporters. The records of Monmouthshire County Council show that in 1911 there was a crisis over the minimum wage to be paid to roadmen in which the ILP representatives were defeated and the Liberals, led by Tom Richards, won the day.

26 There is now no trace of this verse.

27 The Irish Revival, combining as it did a literary movement with political independence, was a great stimulus to MacDiarmid's own national ambitions.

28 During this period, through his association with the Fabians, MacDiarmid did research into the agricultural problems in Scotland and his contribution was acknowledged in Henry D Harben's *The Rural Problem* (1913), p. vi.

29 In 1912 MacDiarmid joined the staff of the *Clydebank and Renfrew Press*.

30 James Maxton (1885-1946), b. Glasgow. A staunch supporter of the ILP and a radical socialist, during the First World War he and MacLean were imprisoned for inciting shipyard workers on Clydeside to strike. Released after the war, Maxton went on to have a distinguished political career. In 1922 he was elected MP for Bridgeton, a seat he held until his death. In 1926 he was elected Chairman of the ILP and remained a radical fighter for working-class rights.

31 John MacLean (1879-1923), b. Pollokshaws, near Glasgow. MacLean was one of the first Communists to make an impact on the British political scene. He was a school teacher who had a reputation as a powerful orator and an educator in Marxist principles, so much so that he was imprisoned for sedition during the First World War. Following the Bolshevik Revolution he was appointed Bolshevik Consul in Glasgow and was, together with Lenin and Trotsky, Honorary President of the First All Russian Congress of Soviets. His health was broken by his imprisonment and his early death was seen as a great blow to the movement he championed. *See* 'John MacLean', *C.P.* I, p 485.

32 Andrew Graham Grieve (1894-1973), MacDiarmid's younger brother. He rose to a position of responsibility in the Inland Revenue Service, moving eventually with his family to London. Although he wrote some poetry, the brothers did not share the same interests and MacDiarmid's extreme opinions often brought them into conflict.

33 Cupar—a small town on the East coast, ten miles south west of Dundee.

34 Unidentified.

35 Forfar—a market town thirteen miles north east of Dundee. MacDiarmid moved there in 1913 and worked for a time on the *Forfar Review*.

36 At Broughton he had joined the Territorial 3rd Lowland Field Ambulance.

37 MacDiarmid was plagued with malaria during and after his war service and was to
    be invalided to malaria camps several times.
38 Eleutherios Venizelos (1864–1936), Prime Minister of Greece from 1910–15, 1924,
    1928–32 and 1933. His sympathy with the Allied cause clashed with that of King
    Constantine. In 1917 Venizelos succeeded in establishing a provisional government at
    Salonika and forced the king's abdication.
39 ? Enver Pasha (1881–1922). Leader in 1908 of the Turkish Revolution and minister
    for war in 1914. After 1918 he fled to Russia and was killed in an insurrection in
    Turkestan.
40 Miss Nellie Murray, see letter 28 April 1918, where she is referred to as 'teaching in
    Essex'.
41 Peter Ross, Maths Master at Broughton (see letter August 1911?). He was killed in
    action in France in July 1916. Tommy Clow and Hector Sutherland were
    schoolmates and as they are here mentioned with Mr Ross, it seems likely that they
    too were killed in the war.
42 Jimmie Westwood, Thomas G P Walker, James Templeton and Simpson were all on
    active service.
43 Dr Drummond was minister at Lothian Road Church (now the Edinburgh
    Filmhouse). MacDiarmid had some association with the church, possibly because it
    had a debating society, while he was at Broughton. The honour awarded to the
    minister's son seems likely to have been a war decoration.
44 Headmaster at Broughton Junior Student Centre, he had retired in 1916.
45 MacDiarmid was editor of *Broughton Magazine in 1910*.
46 The school Literary Society which Ogilvie had inaugurated and of which
    MacDiarmid had been an enthusiastic member.

Somewhere in the East

2 September 1916

Dear Mr Ogilvie

Why it should be vitally necessary for me to write you tonight I can no more
indicate that [than] I can indicate, why, having unaccountably delayed in writing
to you, I found it increasingly and finally absolutely impossible to write to you
again. The loss has been mine, and an incalculable one. One of the chief
considerations in the psychological tangle from which I have never freed myself
is undoubtedly the fact that I have never done anything worthwhile. I have
nursed my ambitions, dreamed my dreams—and grown older, that is all! Never
a day has passed however but what I have thought of you. Never a day but what
I have said, 'Tomorrow I will write the Fine Thing—then I will write to him
again'. But the tomorrow has never come. I have written and written and great
are the piles of my MSS—but they have never taken the one shape I keep on
hunting for. Someday yet perhaps—!

But in the meantime picture me lying here in the mouth of a tent on a Balkan hillside; looking out over the ancient city of Salonika and its crowded waterways, across the sun-smitten gulf to high Olympus (not so very high, after all—only some 3000 feet).

And despite my booklessness, the total absence of such company as in pre-war days I would have found congenial,—despite the ravages of mosquitoes which have paid me marked attentions since I came here (indeed marked me all over), the huge heat, and the fact that the ground beneath me is one mass of ant-hills— a very moving scene!—I am as healthy as ever I was, and happier than I had ever thought to be.

It is a big hospital, that down below there to which I am attached on the Quartermaster's Staff—a cushie job!—and it will be to say enough concerning the life here, or rather the difficulty of living here, to say that business is brisk.

It is a wonderful place this ancient city with its huge new population of soldiers. So many Scotsmen are here that it has been suggested that it should be called not Thessalonica, but Thistleonica. But that would not be just to our allies. East and West meet and mingle here in an indescribable fashion. Soliders of half-a-dozen different nations fraternize in canteens and cafés. Naturally and necessarily one picks up an incredible polyglottery. Even the coins in one's pockets are representative of almost every nation in Europe.

One wearies here for letters in an unspeakable way. Perhaps you will understand and forgive and write me sometime—that is to say if you can make head or tail out of this extraordinary scribble. My address is 64020 Sergt C M Grieve, RAMC, 42nd General Hospital, British Salonika Force.

Now I must close. At least I have managed to write again. I earnestly hope that this letter will find you in good health and spirits, and that you will be interested a little to hear once more, after a long lapse of time, from your old pupil.

C. M. Grieve

Salonika

4 December 1917

Dear Mr Ogilvie,

I have written you several letters at spaces in the great interval since I last heard from you and in the absence of any reply can only conclude that all of them have been turned into fish-food by the fortunes of war, the only alternative being a fear, which I will not give house-room to, that something has happened to you. But once more in the hope that this time I may circumvent the conspiracy of circumstances—or, alternatively, lay that persistent little ghost of unformulated anxiety (perhaps after all it is your letters to me which have gone astray)—I must scribble a few lines to wish you in time the old old wish of a merry Christmas and a happy New Year.

My malaria which ruined my summer is once more quiescent. It hibernates and is unlikely to give further trouble until the hot weather returns, but another of the endemic diseases of this unnatural country has been playing havoc this last fortnight or so with my debilitated constitution and I am only just pulling myself together and accomplishing what is really one of those feats of physiological acrobatics in which lies the real significance of the 'survival of the fittest'. A few more such successes—and I will be able to survive anything. In a Balkan's *Who's Who* I could safely put down my recreation as 'pathological equilibrism'.

Day succeeds day here in a monotony of existence in which an accident or an air-raid is a God-sent diversion. The anatomical side of life is appallingly obtrusive. Conversation is practically monopolised by indecent discussions of 'how one feels today'.[1] I share to the full 'Erewhon' Butler's[2] revulsion from the tendencies of modern science.

Fortunately I am not without books and paper. Turgenev, Henry James, J. M. Synge,[3] the Georgian Poets,[4] Galsworthy's *Fraternity*,[5] Gilbert Murray's Greek translations, [6] and a few others make me little worlds in my spare time that carnal considerations cannot violate—and for myself I have actually committed to paper in rough draft (which nothing will induce me to put into any more final shape as long as I am in khaki) two one-act plays,[7] some seventy poems,[8] and the first volume of a trilogy of autobiographic novels somewhat of a cross in nature between Gorki's *Childhood*,[9] and Wells' *Tono-Bungay*[10]—eheu! I shall arrive yet if I come scatheless out of the holocaust into civil life, where there are personal rights again.

I hope time is being good to you and that I shall have news of you again some happy day at no too great distance.

I wish you all good and desirable things and ascribe myself in affectionate respect,

Your Old Pupil.

C M Grieve.

Please remember me seasonably to Dr Drummond should you be seeing him.

NOTES

1 MacDiarmid was probably writing from a convalescent camp. *See* letter which follows.
2 Samuel Butler (1835–1902), *Erewhon* (1872). The title is an inversion of nowhere and is a satire on utopias.
3 Ivan Turgenev (1818–83), Henry James (1843–1916), John Millington Synge (1871–1909).,
4 The name given to those poets included in Edward Marsh's anthologies of contemporary verse published between 1912 and 1922. Contributors included Sturge Moore, Rupert Brooke, D H Lawrence, Harold Munro, John Collings Squire and many others. Initially drawn to the Georgians, MacDiarmid was to model his *Northern Numbers* on Marsh's anthologies.
5 John Galsworthy (1867–1933), *Fraternity* (1909).
6 Gilbert Murray (1866–1957). Classical scholar and Regius Professor of Greek at Oxford 1908–36, noted for his editions and translations of the Greek dramatists and his literary and social criticism. He had been one of Ogilvie's professors at Glasgow University.
7 One of which was possibly *Nisbet*?
8 During this period MacDiarmid wrote a series of poems which he was to refer to as both 'A Voice from Macedonia' and 'Salonika Poems'. *See also* letter 28 April 1918.
9 Maxim Gorki (1868–1936) (Pseudonym of Alexsei Maksimovich Peshkov). Russian writer whose autobiographical *Childhood* (1913–14) is considered one of his masterpieces.
10 Herbert George Wells (1866–1946). *Tono–Bungay* (1909) is written in first person narrator form and is one of Wells's more experimental works.

The following letter is from the Christmas 1917 edition of *Broughton Magazine* and is an excerpt from one of MacDiarmid's letters to Ogilvie which is not part of the collection in the National Library of Scotland. The introduction states that the letter is from a former pupil who is 'in a rest camp in the East'.

Dear Mr————,

Camped on a high and airy promontory jutting out into the blue Aegean, across which, a day's sail away, my usual station is on a very clear day dimly discernible on a further coast. I am at present enjoying a rest-cure and write in a holiday mood for the first time in close on fifteen months.

A recent recurrence of malignant malaria left me deplorably reduced in physique and stamina and, noting my debility, the authorities took compassion on me and sent me hither to this 'change of air camp' for a ten-days' spell, of which four or five days have still to run.

There are caller air[s] which would revive me more speedily and thoroughly, I know, but failing these yet awhile (the wheels of the chariots of Mars stand badly in need of oiling), the change here is doing me a world of good—I feel a different fellow already—and by the time my holiday is over I should be quite built up again for the winter. Now that the colder weather is setting in I need fear no further recurrence of the fever till next summer by which time I hope to have shaken the dust of Macedon off my Army Pattern boots finally and forever—but one never can tell.

In the meantime, however, I have little to do but eat, sleep, bathe and remember old friends. The bathing is splendid, along a long sweep of beach (reached by a break-neck goats' track down steep cliffs) in waters clear to a great depth and with a fine smooth, sandy bottom. On walking along the shore one may see some quaint native fisheries, with two rickety ladder erections sticking up out of the water like the skeletons of stupendous cranes. From seats on the top of these the fishermen can see their prey entering their nets some distance out. They then haul up the nets until they go out and secure their yield in a primitive old boat. Red mullet, for the most part, and an eel-like fish with silver belly and bright green back, and curious thin sword-like mouths, like a snipe's bill.

More curious still is a chance encounter with a lonely but well-contented Scots highlander, line-fishing with an old cod-hook, baited with the entrails of mussels (with which the adjacent rocks are plentifully bestruck). He has a true highland knack of casting—power to his elbow!—and is doing great damage to a school of pink-and-silvery, flounder-like fish. But as he says, no doubt he'd be 'nane the waur o' a wheen worms'.[1]

But mostly I lie on the cliff-top—the climb back from the beach liking me not—lie in the sunshine on almost bentless terrain, watching the crafts go up and down the shining waterways. All kinds and conditions of vessels are here. Modern men-of-war and motor-craft: old-fashioned sailing-ships and native boats, Trireme and Submarine, galleon and collier, schooner and motor-yacht pass and repass in striking epitomes of naval history.[2]

Behind, the ground rolls endlessly in almost desert stretches. Scarcely a tree is to be seen. But all that Masefield in his *Gallipoli*[3] says of Mudros and the Dardanelles, and the magic colours, which the powerful sunlight draws out of the rocky barrennesses there, is true also of my present location—and even Masefield's pen has not done full justice to the subtle wonders of these unsuspected colours that make it seem as if the wizardry of the slanting rays of the sun turned grey stone and brown clay into gold and silver and ruby and emerald.

And in such settings I lie and dream.

Your old pupil,

C M Grieve.

NOTES

1 'None the worse for a few worms.'
2 During the civil unrest in Greece allied warships were sent to Salonika.
3 John Masefield (1878–1967). *Gallipoli* (1916) is a defence of General Sir Ian Hamilton's disastrous Dardanelles campaign.

Macedonia

13 February 1918

Dear Mr Ogilvie,

My state of mind at this writing can be best indicated perhaps by the following quotations from my current Suggestion Book: viz 'NB—See October 1917, *Little Review*, not allowed to be issued in America, on account of Wyndham Lewis's "Cantleman's Spring Mate".[1] The case of 'Cantleman' was taken into court in New York and brilliantly and humorously defended, but to no avail. The soldier Cantleman and the girl he met in the forest are still most damnably "wrapt in mystery"'—'Scots Bureau. 27/7. (a reference number, which must go as merely adumbrating an extraordinary system I have evolved for not losing sight of workable material concerning Things Scottish—similar systems cover my other interests)—Mr J A Ferguson,[2] sportsman, dramatist, novelist and poet. *Campbell of Kilmohr*.'—'NB T W H Crosland's[3] *The English Sonnet*.'—There are thousands of such entries now in these suggestion books of mine, each indicating some line of creative endeavour, or journalistic intention. Will I ever be free to develop them? Looking over them I can only ejaculate Eureka, Zeugma, Catachresis and all abominable things. I feel like a buried city.

The first thing I must do when I get into civilian clothes again is to go into a comtee. of Ways and Means. Then, if the way is clear, I must first of all, however intriguing other speculations may be, dispose of my trilogy of novels. I could complete them in a year. My brother is now 1st Clerk in the 4th Inland Revenue Division, Edinburgh—I will live on him for that year, probably. After that I can work up these Suggestion Books—and my Catholic Adventures—and the one-act plays and poems.—The appalling thing is that there are additions every day to these Suggestion Books, new impulses for lyrics, new motifs—and I can finish nothing under present circumstances—and I have already mortgaged more than my allotted span several times over. Verily as some one said, 'Life is a predicament in which we find ourselves before death.'[4]

I was glad to get your last letter. (I forget whether I have written you since receiving it or not). I remember Roderick Kerr[5] well—He succeeded me as editor of the Mag didn't he?—and went in for punning verse after Thomas Hood.[6] I should like to see his *English Review* stuff.[7] If you should be writing to him please congratulate him on my behalf on his 'arrival'. I shall hope someday to meet him, as you suggest the fates may allow, chez vous. Other Edinburgh news is scanty. Nisbet's sister has just been married. I am afraid that by the time I get back all the nice girls will be bespoken. Still we have our compensations here. One Maregena, A Spanish girl hailing from Barcelona,[8] would interest you. Only a Turgenev could write her up. Incidentally she writes herself. Curiously poignant little songs they are, somewhat like Heine's or Emily Dickinson's. I am collecting all she will permit to pass into my hands. One day I shall translate them perhaps. – – – There are others. – – – Miss Murray is teaching down in Essex now. A friend of mine, a *New Age* writer and poet, lives there too in the same village—G Reston Malloch.[9] And Miss Cecilia Murray is down in Bucks.[10]

I am in excellent health just now and having a fairly lively time. We had a champion Burns' Night, the 'Immortal Memory' devolving upon me. I do a lot of talking and speechifying. Modern musical tendencies was the theme of a lively discussion the other night: but when we got off generalities and down to names and motifs, I found that Rimsky-Karasov [*sic*], Stravinsky and Debussy did not enter into the scheme of things for the others, so I dropped out. The general ignorance of recent stringed-instrument experimentation is abysmal—and yet a fellow who can sing 'Annie Laurie' or has heard of Chopin and Handel contests my right to argue seeing I do not like music and am tone deaf. A mad world!

It is a terrible thought, shutting me in most horribly on myself, that of a list of say twelve people in whom I am for the moment pre-eminently interested, not one of them is known to any other member of the mess—these are Paul Fort,[11] the Sitwells,[12] Rebecca West,[13] Serge Asanoff,[14] Remy de Goncourt [Remy de Gourmont?][15] (whose posthumous papers I am dying to read), Joyce Kilmer[6] (an admirable appreciation of whose works I have just read in *The Month*), Theodore Maynard[17] (quotations from whose *Drums of Defeat*—and in extenso his fine tribute to Padraic Pearse[18]—I find in the latest *Dublin Leader*, the Sinn Fein paper, to hand)—and so on.

Still one can always read. Under my pillow just now I have Chesterton's *Club of Queer Trades*,[19] Alpha of the Plough's *Pebbles on the Shore*,[20] E V Lucas's *A Little of Everything*,[21] some *English Reviews*[22] containing stories by Caradoc Evans,[23] some copies of *Everyman* and of *The Month* and *The Tablet* and *The New York Saturday Post* and *The Sydney Bulletin* and *Life* and *La Revue Franco-Macedoniene*, and some *National News*,[24] copies with instalments of Wells' *Soul of a Bishop*,[25]—on the whole I cannot complain.

I have a letter from the Rev T S Cairncross[26]—did I ever mention him to you? He has published several volumes of pleasant prose and two volumes of poetry: *The Margin of Rest* (Elkin Matthews), written largely under the influence of Heine on the one hand and Bliss Carman[27] on the other, and *The Masters' Return* (Scott), a volume of rhymeless rhythms reminiscent of Henley.[28] He could not be omitted from any adequate anthology of modern Scottish poetry. Several of his vernacular ballads are wonderfully good. But the great bulk of his stuff is still in MSS. He is just back from chaplaining in France and is likely to contribute something good to the literature of the War. I should like to send on some of his stuff to you—but must wait till I get home. I should like your opinion of him. He writes most delightful letters.

Excuse this paper and scribbling hand. I shall hope to hear from you again soon. It was fine of you to will my safe return. Any psychological force I can support the suggestion with, will be devoted to making you an effective master of Nietzschean methods.[29]

Au revoir, then, with all good wishes.

Yours etc.

C M Grieve.

PS   Please remember me to the Rev Dr Drummond.

NOTES

1   Percy Wyndham Lewis (1884–1957), English artist, writer and critic. Co-editor with Ezra Pound of *Blast*. The *Little Review* was published in New York and described itself as a 'Magazine of the Arts: Making no Compromise with Public Taste'. The short story referred to became the subject of controversy when the Post Office refused to distribute the periodical through the mail on the grounds that they judged this story to be obscene. The matter was taken to court but judgement was made against the periodical. It is difficult to see what could have aroused such a reaction to the story, which deals with a love relationship in wartime and ends ambiguously, but the judge in summing up the case stated that 'the details of the sex relations are set forth to attract readers to the story because of their salacious character'.

2   John Alexander Ferguson (1879–1928). Scottish poet, author and editor, he worked most of his life as an agent of the National Bank of Scotland at Stirling. He first published his volume of sonnets, *Thyrea*, in 1912, a collection much admired by MacDiarmid and which he recognised as representing a new and modern spirit in Scottish poetry. *Campbell of Kilmohr* (1915) is a drama in Scots. Ferguson also edited the *Fortnightly Review*. MacDiarmid and he became great friends in the post-war period and Ferguson contributed to all three of the *N.N.* series. *See* MacDiarmid's articles on his work in *S.C.*, August 1922, p 24 and *C.S.S.*, pp 1–2.

3   Thomas William Hodgson Crosland (b. 1868), English editor and critic. *The English Sonnet* (1917).

4   ?George Santayana's *Articles and Essays*: 'Life is not a spectacle or a feast, it is a predicament'.

5   Roderick Watson Kerr (1893–1960). Another talented Broughtonian who came under Ogilvie's influence. He became sub-editor of the *Liverpool Post* and, together with two other Broughtonians—John Gould and John Malcolm Thomas—founded the Porpoise Press.

6   Thomas Hood (1799–1845), English poet and humorist.

7   Kerr had had several of his war poems published in *The English Review*.

8   *See* 'Spanish Girl', *C.P.* I, 10–13.

9   George Reston Malloch (1875–1953). Scottish poet, dramatist and journalist, he wrote in English and Scots. He contributed to *N.N.* and *S.C.* and was drama critic for MacDiarmid's *The Scottish Nation*. His works include *Lyrics and other Verses* (1913), *Poems and Lyrics* (1917), *The Birthright* (1912) and *Arabella* (1913), the last two being dramas. *See* MacDiarmid's article on Malloch in *C.S.S.*, pp 35–7.

10 Another friend from his Broughton days?

11 Paul Fort (1872–1960), contemporary French *vers libriste*.

12 Edith (1887–1964), Osbert (1892–1969) and Sacheverell (b. 1897) Sitwell.

13 Rebecca West (1892–1983), pen-name from Ibsen's *Rosmersholm* of Cicily Isabel Fairfield. *See* MacDiarmid's review of her *The Judge* (1922) in *S.C.*, September 1922, pp 59–60 and his 'Following Rebecca West in Edinburgh', *S.C.*, October 1922, pp 69–73.

14 ?Sergei Aksakov (1791–1859), Russian writer noted mainly for his *Years of Childhood* (1856) a work which chronicled life on a provincial estate in Russia.

15 Remy de Gourmont (1858–1915), French symbolist poet, novelist and critic.

16 Joyce Kilmer (1886–1918), American poet and critic, author of the popular poem, 'A Tree'. The article 'Joyce Kilmer: An Appreciation' by Hugh Anthony Allan appeared in *The Month* (a Catholic review of literature, science and art), May 1917, pp 399–406.

17 Theodore Maynard (1890–1956), English poet and author. *Drums of Defeat and other Poems* (1917). His poem, 'To the Irish Dead', appeared in the *Dublin Leader*, 2 February 1918, p 630. The *Dublin Leader* was owned and edited by David Patrick Moran (1871–1936). Initially a strong influence on the independence movement, this periodical subsequently became the organ of the Irish nationalist party, the Sinn Fein.

18 Padraic Pearse (1879–1916), Irish poet and nationalist. Founder of the Irish Gaelic Revival, Pearse had joined the Irish Republican Brotherhood (later the Irish Republican Army) and led them in the Easter Rising of 1916.

19 Gilbert Keith Chesterton (1874–1936), *The Club of Queer Trades* (1906).

20 *Pebbles on the Shore* (1917). *See also* letter 20 August 1916.

21 Edward Verrall Lucas (1868–1938). English essayist and biographer and assistant editor of *Punch. A Little of Everything* (1912).

22 *The English Review*, a weekly 'devoted to the arts, to letters and ideas', started and edited by Ford Madox Ford (Hueffer) in London in 1908. It was one of the most important literary periodicals of its day. D H Lawrence's work was first published there and he contributed to it for many years. Other contributors included Conrad, Hardy, James, H G Wells, R B Cunninghame Graham and almost every writer of note in that period.

23 Caradoc Evans (pseudonym of David Evans) (1878–1945), Welsh writer known for his short stories about rural life.

24 *Everyman*, a weekly review of literature and international politics, published in London, 1912–1920. *The Tablet* (like *The Month*) a Catholic journal published in London. *The New York Saturday Post* [Review?], a weekly review of science, art, literature and drama. *The Sydney Bulletin*, an Australian national journal which promoted the work of native writers. *Life*, a weekly published in London. *La Revue Franco-Macedoniene*, a monthly published by 'les officiers, sous-officiers et soldats de

l'Armée d' Orient' in Salonika during the First World War. It included articles, poems, regimental news and progress reports on the war. *The National News*, a weekly newspaper published in London from 1917–1921.

25 Published in 1917.

26 Thomas Scott Cairncross (1872–1919). MacDiarmid knew him from Langholm where he was minister of Langholm South United Free Church. He had written a novel in Scots—*Blawearie* (1911)—and published poems in Scots and English in *The Margin of Rest* (1904) and *The Return of the Master* (1905).

27 William Bliss Carman (1861–1929), Canadian poet noted for his nature poetry. *Collected Poems* (1905).

28 William Ernest Henley (1849–1903). English poet, playwright and critic who met and became friendly with Robert Louis Stevenson while he was being treated at Edinburgh Royal Infirmary. His work, particularly his 'hospital' poems, is noted for its realism. He was also an early experimenter in free verse. *Collected Poems* (1898), *Hawthorn and Lavender* (1901), *A Song of Speed* (1903).

29 Like so many other writers of the period (Yeats , Shaw, John Davidson, Edwin Muir) MacDiarmid was greatly influenced by Nietzsche's ideas, mainly through *The New Age* where Orage had been promoting Nietzsche's work from 1907 on. MacDiarmid was much in sympathy with the philosopher's conception of the links between nature, consciousness and language (set out in *The Birth of Tragedy*) and certainly supported Nietzsche's view of the artist as a revolutionary of the spirit. However, as the above comment indicates, MacDiarmid was also capable of an ironic detachment, something which saved him from the excesses of discipleship.

Macedonia

28 April 1918

Dear Mr Ogilvie:-

Yours of date a month ago today just to hand by a mail which yielded me nothing else. The postal authorities have been dealing hardly with me lately. I have had no letters from home since 2/3/18. Imagine then the doubled joy with which I welcomed your letter.

I do not think I have ever felt better since the malaria microbe invaded my veins way back in September 1916 than I do at this writing. During the past fortnight or so I have been constantly in the open sharing all the strenuousness that is involved in the establishing of a new camp. I have experienced the sundry travails of a heavy porter, a navvy, a general contractor's ganger—and, if the weather has been progressively hot, well the good brown ale at intervals has been all the more refreshing. Our labours are nearly over. Soon we will resume the ordinary routine. But it has been good while it has lasted—hard work, long hours, willing comrades, a little period of hard playing and riotous fun, and then, the soundest of sleep.

Beneath my newly reissued solar topee my face is of a deep good-natured brown and there are no dark rings under the eyes which are clearer and livelier perhaps than lately they were. Something deep in me has been stirred by the sensation of striving muscles and the sight of spaded clay that never responds to the disciplined system of more settled periods. Once but for my father (and that was after I had been to Broughton a year or so) I would have become a gardener – – – but that was so many centuries ago!

I wish I could lay my hands just now on Maurice Hewlett's *Epic of Hodge*.[1] I am just in the mood to appreciate it. As it is I shall be surprised if I do not find it to my hand any moment. I nearly always do. You comment on the strange way in which I seem to keep in touch. I suppose it is the operation of some law similar to that which makes birds of a feather flock together. Seek and you shall find—such urgent need as mine cannot be denied. Just now I have in my little Nestlé's Milk Box library a recent number of the *Dublin Review*,[2] Viola Meynell's *Lot Barrow*,[3] Stella Callaghan's *Vision*,[4] Turgenev's *Rudin* in Constance Garnett's translation,[5] Austin Dobson's *Fielding*,[6] a monograph on Landseer,[7] Archibald Marshall's *Richard Baldock*,[8] a presentation copy autographed by the author to his friend, Dion Clayton Calthorp[9] [*sic*], whom we also know, and a copy of the *Englishwoman*[10] containing a very delightful review of the poems of George Reston Malloch[11] (erstwhile the G R M of the 'Ham and Meat' corner of the *Glasgow Herald*) who is one of my own correspondents too. – – – It is strange, but it could not have been otherwise if I had been in the middle of the Sahara. At the worst I would have written (or more probably dreamt) my own library. – – And it may further interest you to know that most of my reading comes from 'The Soldiers' Recreation Fund, 29 Drumsheugh Gardens, Edinburgh'.

I am in one of my buoyant moods. When I wrote that last letter in which I despaired of ever producing anything I was in a 'Rudin' mood—but today! No, I will not be snowed under in any mental sense. What I do most desperately fear is that my physique will not carry me through, or that the free expression of myself will be inhibited by family and economic cares before I get a chance to establish myself in a monetary sense—which I must do before I can labour uninterruptedly and successfully at my work.—But today I am well in body and in mind and all my diverse purposes are grouping themselves harmoniously into a delectable life's work with no confusion or failure anywhere: – – If only the war would end soon and let me get begun in real earnest!

In a day or two per registered post I shall send on to you a series of poems designed to fill a gap in the Soldier Poets' series published by Erskine MacDonald, which so far has mainly consisted of the work of men serving on the Western Front and at all events has not so far included anything from Salonika. I suggest calling the little collection 'A Voice from Macedonia'.[12]

They represent the work of three consecutive days, except one or two written earlier and at isolated times. Probably they might be the better of having more time spent on them but that would be rather against the idea of 'soldier-verse'— essentially a hasty and spontaneous thing. But I send them to you, rather than directly to Erskine MacDonald's, confident that I am not trespassing too far on your kindness in asking you to read them first and make any little alterations or corrections you deem good. Will you please then submit them to Erskine MacDonald for me?[13] I can guarantee a circulation of at least 100 among my own immediate friends here—and advts. in the *Balkan News*[14] and the *RAMC Corps Magazine*[15] would be profitable, while of course I have at least 50 personal friends at home who would have a copy.

Whatever happens to them I feel sure you will find some interest in these Active Service effusions and that in itself will amply redeem the few leisure hours they took to write. I heard that you utilised my Karabouroun letter[16] for the B.M. and if any of these poems can be similarly used I shall be only too happy. It was, by the way, with remarkable indirectness through a Miss Mabel Leighton, now teaching at Ayton in Berwickshire, that I heard of my reappearance in the B.M. She it seems knew me at Broughton. I do not remember her at all—but how nice to be remembered after all this time!

I have been definitely passed for invaliding home as a chronic malaria subject. The scheme was temporarily hung up but has just restarted. So expect a surprise call from me sometime during this summer!

I shall ask my mother in my next letter to post on to you two or three volumes of Cairncross's work I happen to have lying at home.

You refer to my letters showing a 'serene detachment from the War'—but please remember the strictness of the Censorship. However loyal I may be to certain ideals bound up in the Allied Cause I was never to say the least of it an Anglophile—and when I am free of his majesty's uniform again I shall have a very great deal indeed to say and to write that I have not nearly enough desire for premature and secret martyrdom to say or write until then.

In a postscript you ask me to give you my full denomination and address in this reply but your doubts seem to be groundless—you have correctly addressed me on this last envelope.

By the way if you hear anything about Miss Murray[17]—more particularly in regard to her health—please tell me. We write—but the intervals are always long and irregular. The last time I heard from her she was teaching down in Essex. I have not heard from her now for more than usually long—which generally means that she has had another breakdown. She scarcely ever alludes to such matters herself and after inexplicable silences resumes as casually as if she had never left of[f] writing. I am not now in touch with anyone who is in the way of hearing anything about her, but at Broughton you may be. I am afraid my relations with the other sex are incredibly complicated and that between Nelly and I, if it could be written up, would be voted quite impossible, but it is nevertheless although so sketchy and haphazard vital in different way to both of us—and part and parcel, as you say, of a group of associations I would not willingly let die.

Now I must cease. I shall post the poems on as soon as I can get them censored. Hoping to hear from you soon again—and ever with the kindest regards.

Yours.

C M Grieve.

NOTES

1   Maurice Hewlett (1861–1923), English novelist, poet and essayist. The work MacDiarmid is referring to is entitled *The Song of the Plow* (1916), an epic of England from the Norman Conquest, in which Hodge is the Everyman character. The work is interesting for its use of dialect and archaic words.

2   Initially a monthly review of the arts and current affairs and then was incorporated into *The Month*.

3   Viola Meynell (1885–1956), daughter of Alice Meynell and noted for her biography of her mother. *Lot Barrow* (1913).

4   *A Vision*, published in 1913.

5   Translated by Constance Garnett in 1918.

6   Henry Austin Dobson (1840–1921), English poet. His monograph of Fielding was published in 1883.

7   Edwin Henry Landseer (1802–73). English artist famous for his paintings of animals, particularly that of the highland stag in a Scottish landscape, entitled 'Monarch of the Glen'.

8   Archibald Marshall (1866–1934). English novelist, short-story writer and humorist. *Richard Baldock* (1906).

9   Dion Clayton Calthrop (1878–1937), English artist and author.

10   *The Englishwoman*, a quarterly review of the arts, published in London.

11   A review of his *Poems and Lyrics* (1917) was published in the April-June 1917, pp 87–8, edition of *The Englishwoman*. The 'Ham and Meat' feature of the *Glasgow Herald* printed poems and prose pieces daily.

12   *See* letter 4 December 1917.

13   Erskine MacDonald accepted this work, but MacDiarmid became impatient and withdrew it, hoping to place it with Nelson through his contact with John Buchan, but that too only led to a deferred offer of help. Poems from this collection were however published in *Broughton Magazine*, Summer 1919. Referred to there as 'Salonika Poems', they included 'To a French Girl Friend' and 'Beyond Exile'.

14   *The Balkan News*, published in Salonika from 1915–19 for the 'British Army in Macedonia', it contained war and army news, light verse, anecdotes, etc.

15   *Journal of the Royal Army Medical Corps*, published monthly giving mainly medical and corps news.

16   *See* letter Christmas 1917. The Greek fortress at Kara Burun on the east side of the Salonikan Gulf, fifteen miles from the city, was the location of British Headquarters. Given the content of the letter written from there it probably was also the main medical and convalescent centre.

17   Miss Nelly Murray.

There is a six months gap in the correspondence at this point. During this period MacDiarmid had continued to suffer badly from malaria and had been invalided home at one point. It was during this stretch at home that he married Margaret Skinner (on 13 June 1918).

When MacDiarmid returned to service, he moved with his unit to France. The Allied Forces had launched the Somme Offensive on 21 March 1918 and thereafter action on the Western Front accelerated. Sometime prior to Armistice Day, MacDairmid was transferred to a malaria camp near Dieppe, but by December 1918 he had been moved on service to Sections Lahore Indian General Hospital at Marseilles, a native hospital for East Indians set up to deal mainly with those suffering from mental disturbances, where he was to remain until he was demobbed in the summer of 1919.

The letter which follows was written as a response to the termination of hostilities.

Somewhere in France [Dieppe?][1]

11 November 1918

Dear Mr Ogilvie,

It is some time now since I wrote you: but you will understand that I have had a somewhat busy time of late. I called down to see you at Broughton when I was on final leave but you were off ill and I had not time to come to your house. Shortly afterwards I was transported hither—to a great malaria concentration camp for a further course of treatment so-called. Conditions are somewhat rough and we are kept pretty well at it. Still I am A1, or rather B1. What leisure I do get I am devoting to giving courses of lectures on 'Political and Commercial Geography' and 'Civics and Town Planning' under the Army Educational Scheme. These monopolise three nights a week. I had little thought to return to teaching but the work is absorbing and I think greatly worth while.

News came today of the cessation of hostilities. It was taken very very quietly—incalculable relief but no mafficking. Technically we are still invalids and may be sent home and demobilised all the sooner on that ground. Anyhow it is splendid knowing that the duration is over and that one is at last actually on the last lap.

My plans for after the war are all cut and fried—I am ready and eager for a time of systematic production. But I shall hope to talk all my plans over with you and I know that whatever I write you will give me the benefit of your advice and experience.

My present address is:- 64020 Sergt C M Grieve, RAMC, No. 3 Group, Reception Camp, No. 2 L. of C. Area, B.E. F., France.

I hope your home has escaped the ravages of the 'flu epidemic[2] and that you soon recovered from the indisposition you were suffering from when I was last in Edinr.

Please give my kindest regards to Mrs Ogilvie and the children. I hope this will find you all well in health and spirits.

With all good wishes.

Chris.

NOTES

1 *See* letter 27 December 1918 where MacDiarmid refers to having been in the vicinity of Dieppe.
2 1918 Spanish influenza epidemic which claimed more people than the total casualties of the war.

Somewhere in France

24 November 1918

Dear Mr Ogilvie:-

Your delightful letter to hand! It redeemed for me the unspeakable unprofitableness of a cold dull Sunday forenoon when I was vainly and with a stultifying sense of unworthiness endeavouring to mitigate my bleak untidy boredom by perusing the current issues of *La Vie Parisienne*[1] and *Le Rire.*[2] Forthwith, as a sign of my gratitude, I am going to scribble some sort of a return, for the inadequacy of which please blame my cramping comfortless circumstances. I am half-recumbent on damp and muddy tentboards, with blankets, slarried over with mud, wrapped round ice-cold feet, and unobliging vertebrae dove-tailing unevenly into the humps and hollows of a stack of miscellaneous kit, while a woodfire in a biscuit-tin brazier flames and smokes unequally and disconcertingly in the mouth of the tent. Some setting!

I was greatly interested in what you say of the termination of hostilities and the future you forecast. I myself believe that we have lost this war—in everything but actuality! When I see scores of sheep go to a slaughter house I do not feel constrained to admire their resignation. Nor do I believe that the majority of soldiers killed were sufficiently actuated by ideals or capable of entertaining ideas to justify such terms as 'supreme self-sacrifice, etc.' I have been oppressed by my perception of the wide-spread automatism—fortuity—of these great movements and holocausts. A painter covers a canvas with a number of rapid brush marks—a critic comes along and writes it up at inordinate length, seeing in it all manner of technical and aesthetic qualities which the painter had probably not even the mentality to comprehend. So with 'patriotism'—'a war of ideas'—'democracy versus autocracy' etc. I more and more incline to the belief that human intelligence is a mere by-product of little account—that the purpose and destiny of the human race is something quite apart from it—that religion, civilisation and so forth are mere 'trimmings', irrelevant to the central issues. However I cannot justly present these opinions here nor have I the space or time to show what has led to my forming them. Only, more and more, with Matthew Arnold, do I believe in the necessity for 'keeping aloof from what is called the practical view of things. To try and approach truth from one side after another, not to strive or cry, nor to persist in pressing forward, on any one side, with violence and self-will—it is only thus, it seems to me, that mortals may hope to gain any vision of the mysterious Goddess, whom we shall never see except in outline but only thus even in outline.'[3]

In saying in my last letter that all my plans for the future are cut and dried I should have qualified myself. What I meant was that my life-work is really done—that various books exist complete and unchangeable in my mind—what remains is only to do the actual writing. But alas in real affairs I must condescend to the practical view. It will be necessary for me to do my writing in what leisure and suitable atmosphere will be allowed to me by bread-and-butter employment—and my first duty will be to secure such employment as rapidly as possible in some suitable place. What an odious problem! I do not suppose for a moment that anything really suitable or adequately lucrative will turn up. Fortunately the fact that I am now married does not complicate these difficulties. But we will see in due course.

Did I tell you, by the way, that Colonel John Buchan[4] expressed himself in very laudatory terms concerning my Salonika poems?

Where and how is Kerr? I have not yet contrived to see any of his stuff. Is he still active? I am greatly hoping to meet him in the not-too-distant future.

Please give my kindest regards to Mrs Ogilvie and the children. I hope they are all well and have successfully dodged the 'flu epidemic which has according to the papers been so bad in Edinburgh.

I hope you have completely recovered from your own indisposition.

You were, by the way, wrong in fearing that I had had a relapse of malaria. The phrase which led to the assumption was 'wrot sarcastick'. I am afraid that, the Censorship being still unabated, I cannot make the matter clearer in the meantime. But I am really feeling marvellously fit although conditions here are in every way conducive to an opposite condition.

Hoping to hear from you again as soon as may be, and with all good wishes.

I remain.

C M Grieve.

PS   By the way I wonder (in connection with what you say in your relationship to the newer ideas) if you have read *A Schoolmaster's Diary* by S P B Mais.[5] Carelessly and impetuously written it is yet a mine of good things. I have just ben re-reading it—also Professor Hugh Walker's *Outlines of Victorian Literature*[6]—a glorious textbook.

NOTES

1   *La Vie Parisienne*, one of the first French illustrateds, founded in 1863 as a journal for artists and writers and continued into the early twentieth century.

2   ?*Le Rire*, a journal 'épisodique de la view au front', published by the French Armed Forces during the war years.

3   The quotation 'keeping aloof from what is called the practical view of things' is from Arnold's 'The Function of Criticism', but the lines 'to try and approach truth . . . only thus even in outline' are from the preface to the 1865 edition of *Essays in Criticism*. The whole piece was taken by MacDiarmid from Hugh Walker's *The Literature of the Victorian Era* (*see* note below). Of interest too is Walker's comment on Arnold's 'disinterestedness' (*see* pp 968–9 of Walker's book), for MacDiarmid was to use this criticial concept to explain the kind of impartiality which he claimed was the distinctiveness of the Scottish literary tradition.

4   John Buchan (Lord Tweedsmuir) (1875–1940), Scottish writer and statesman, b. Perth. During World War I he served on HQ staff until 1917 when he became Director of Information. He established his literary popularity through adventure stories: *Prester John* (1910), *The Thirty Nine Steps* (1915), *Greenmantle* (1916).

5   Stuart Peter Brodie Mais (1885–1975), English author, journalist, schoolmaster and broadcaster. *A Schoolmaster's Diary* (1918).

6   Hugh Walker (1855–1939), Professor of English Literature, St David's, Lampeter. *The Literature of the Victorian Era* (1910).

[Letter Heading: Sections Lahore Indian General Hospital, B.E.F. France.]

Marseilles

27 December 1918

Dear Mr Ogilvie:-

I am as happy—or more so—here than I was otherwise when I wrote you last from the wet muddy cold neighbourhood of Dieppe. There are about 30 whites of us attached to the above big native hospital. Four senior NCO's including myself occupy a delightful little flat in a fine old Chateau set on a bluff on the outskirts of the city, overlooking the blue sea, surrounded by sub-tropical woodlands and old orchards and gardens where the red and yellow rosebuds still nod beside the walks and the oranges ripen slowly along the old walls in the strong sunshine. We have little neat bedrooms to ourselves complete with real beds furnished with sheets, mattresses, pillows and all the sumptuous rest of it. One could not be more cushily circumstanced on service. Perhaps I may be a trifle snobbish. But the status of a Sergeant here as Sub-Assistant-Surgeon mark you! instead of mere Wardmaster as in an all-British unit is infinitely satisfactory. Duties are nearly negligible. Routine is so relaxed that the oppression of the system is brought to the irreducible minimum. All discipline except self-discipline is practically non–existent. The old creeper-hung weather-coloured Chateau is a veritable martial Abbey of Thelema.[1]

On the way down I spent a lively day in Paris and in an inadequate transatlantic fashion 'did' most of the 'lions'—but Marseilles for light, life, colour, music, gaiety and danger beats Paris hollow and I am revelling in its cosmopolitan excitements under the expert guidance of a young French lady who speaks four languages and is capable of brains and beauty in each of them, and who is attached to the Norwegian Consulate here. In her company I kept the fête de Nöel in quicksilver fashion. May no birds migrate to Gath![2] Suffice it to say that in the perfecting of my dexterity in the sweet Provençal patois and in penetrating the warm secrets of Southern life my volatile temperament is running with the swift delightful smoothness of a high-grade electrical contrivance: and once again I take as my temporary motto:—'It is better to be an electric current for five years than a vegetable for fifty'. The dilly-dally policy in demobilisation ceases to worry me.

Just before I came south your letter of Dec. 14th arrived. I read it in the Boulogne-Paris express—with enormous amusement and underlying impotent contempt at my own epistolary antics and no little dismay on fresh realization of all I really owe you. What leads me to write—above all to you—as I sometimes do I cannot imagine—no sooner is the unspeakable missive irretrievably dispatched than I realize its unutterable crudity, its unfathomable failure in expression of the real content of my mind! However your gentle irony shows unfailing understanding and my own keen appreciation of the Anatole France[3] quality of your reply shows that I am not unutterably lost myself—to what? There's the rub.

I was certainly in a dreadful condition of mind when I wrote last. No fit of 'blues' approaching that in prolonged intensity has ever visited me before[4]—nor have I often lost my deliberate pose of depersonalization so completely. My state amounted to cerebral neuritis almost. However it is over. I regained myself by using my natural safety-valve and the result which I am busily licking into shape is a sheaf of studies similar in angle of approach to 'Cerebral'[5] but dealing with diverse psychological crises and reactions. – – But you shall read them at the earliest possible moment, as soon as I have purified and concentrated their excellent fury.

But that in my ineffably disconnected fashion I am not at all blind to certain boon qualities in your wonderful letters let me quote what my wife said of your last (I sent it to her—I hope you do not mind my doing so—because of its own real interest and because my experimental habit found a congenial speculative field in the possible interactions of her own thought and yours in regard to my own vagaries). She wrote—she is of course very young and instinct with a rectitude I have none of—'Surely, Chris, you *cannot* fail when you have such a friend to trust in you and help you.' It is significant that even she should cast the sentence in interrogative form. Apart from that it shows that even to one, who knows me only slightly and you only by hearing me speaking of you, your perfect friendliness is evident. I may be unable to express myself normally and tactfully on such matters—but I want you to know that I do fully realize the spirit in which you write and hold our correspondence far from lightly.

Apart from that, however, I was enormously struck by your uncanny divination of the extraordinary possibility that I may 'disappear' again. I too recognise that it is possible—even, under certain circumstances, highly probable. Yet I cannot explain. To do so (not explain—but disappear) will be black ingratitude to you and a matter of infinite impotent regret to myself. But in such matters I am not the captain of my fate.[6] However I promise to resist this inexplicable tendency to the full. If our relationship was a blood one or a business one or mainly one of ordinary friendship I am bound to confess that in all likelihood it would be impossible for me to organise myself as an active agent in the maintenance of any continuity or comprehensibility of intercourse actual or epistolary—but fortunately it is not so, and I will endeavour, with an uneasy sense that you are having an uncommonly bad bargain of it, to evince a fidelity real enough if incurably erratic and to avoid the all-besetting tangents of unintelligibility as far as possible.

However your anticipation of the possibility of my 'disappearance' shows a far-going understanding which I will happily be able to count on as an advocate against my unavoidable self-accusations of unaccountable baseness.

Please transmit to Kerr my congratulations on his M.C. and hopes for his speedy recovery. I shall look forward eagerly to seeing his book.[7] No, Buchan does not read for Lane now—he is one of Nelson's directors.[8] Erskine MacDonald after as I told you provisionally accepting my stuff wrote that he found it impossible to put on the market for perhaps an indefinite interval so I withdrew the MSS—sent them to Buchan who seemed enthusiastic about some of them but was only able to promise after-the-war help: so I have done nothing further. My only disappointment lay in the fact that thus whatever happens they lose topicality. However I'm not worrying.

I have now taken careful stock: and have decided not to seek any employment but to sink or fall as a free-lance pure and simple. I have accordingly filled up the necessary papers to secure priority of demob: I may be released in Feb. or March—but I am easy as to that and in the meantime I am, as I have said, writing (as well as living) a lot. Later on we'll see what we'll see.

Please write again whenever you can. I send my kindest regards to Mrs Ogilvie and the children and to yourself, with all seasonable greetings and good wishes,

Yours Sincerely,

C M Grieve.

NOTES

1 Rabelais's Abbey of Thélème in *Gargantua* (1532), the motto of which was 'Fay ce que vouldrais'. The hospital was located at the Château Mirabeau at Estaque near Marseilles.

2 Samuel 1:20. Tell it not in Gath, publish it not in the streets of Askelon. That is, do not spread news of the celebration at home. *See* 'To a French Girl Friend', *C.P.* II, 1202.

3 Anatole France, pseudonym of Anatole François Thibault (1844–1924). French writer noted for his satirical and sceptical works.

4 It is possible that the letter he is referring to is missing from this collection. The letter which precedes the present one is ebullient in tone and has none of the despairing notes MacDiarmid is referring to.

5 Published in *Annals of the Five Senses* (1923).

6 W E Henley's 'Invictus': 'I am the master of my fate, I am the captain of my soul.'

7 Kerr served as an officer with a tank regiment and was awarded the Military Cross. A collection of his verse, *Waur Daubs*, was published by Lane in 1919.

8 Buchan became director of Nelson's in 1903.

Marseilles

23 March 1919

Dear Mr Ogilvie

It is now over a month since I got back to Marseilles and it is high time that I was reporting progress. (But that is not all. My slowness in writing this time has a new and graver aspect. Your last letter, which I received in St Andrews when on leave, established a new relation with new obligations. And this time negligence has a worse complexion of vital inconsideration. Will I never overcome that mastering horror of rational sequence which has lost me already so many good friends, including the person I might have been if my life had ever been susceptible of ordinary order, and made me a sort of stepson of Hagar?[1]— Thus belatedly it would be a further impertinence to essay an expression of gratitude for that letter. I wonder if when Peggy and I saw you in Edinburgh anything in the bearing of either of us told you without words that it had had its ineffaceable effect?)

—I have had a busy month working in my accustomed jungles. I have ceased to marvel at the existence and enormity of them: but am industriously clearing paths. Evidence: (having made Peggy my agent and repository) these all new since I came back, and not drafted or merely noted down for further indefinitely-postponed treatment, but actually completed, worked out at high pressure and yet with all the care and thoroughness I can munster [sic], dismissed from a mind eager to turn to other matters, and signed, sealed and sent home (Peggy can see to the business end of the matters—she has had a sound and well-varied journalistic experience despite her deceptive shyness and 'youngness')—(1) a study of the tech[n]ique and temper of Joseph Conrad's work.[2] (2) a Parisian sketch, designed for the back page of the *Manchester Guardian*. (3) several sketches for a book on 'Marseilles, Moods and Memories' which I am doing in collaboration with one Leon Pavey[3] who has 'appeared' frequently in the *Guardian*, *Punch*, *New Age*, *Passing Show* and other papers (the book consists of 35 sketches—Pavey 20, 12 completed—myself 15, 3 completed and 1 which I am not sure will congenially fit in—but will see): (4) eleven or twelve sets of verses: and (5) a 20,000 word 'book' on 'The Soviet State' comprising (1) A Preface. (2) A selected Bibliography. (3) An account of the present situation in Russia and the Allied attitude thereto. (4) A discussion of the Old Regime and the causes of the Revolution. (5) An account of the development of the Revolution through the Duma Provisional Govt. to the present Soviet Republic. (6) A detailed description of the actual machinery of Bolshevik government.—I have told P. to try and place it with either P S King, Headley Bros or Fifield. Whether she has already sent on 'Salonika Poems' to Lane or not I do not know. I expect she has. She has also on hand a huge unwieldy study called 'Triangular'[4] somewhat after the manner of 'Cerebral' but not episodal.—If *Blast* were still being issued it might appear there. It is an essay in futurism.[5]

The Soviet thing entailed a fearful amount of reading: but I have also found time to read in the original a big anthology of contemporary French poets and am in communication now with Paul Valéry,[6] André Gide,[7] Albert Samhain[8] [*sic*] and a few others endeavouring to secure permission to incorporate translations of certain poems and confessions of faith in an analysis which I propose to write of the motivation and method of modern French creative art.[9]—In this I have been fortunate to secure the help of a really brilliant French girl. I have re-read too with great delight George Moore's *Sister Theresa*[10] [*sic*] and Alfred Oliphant's [*sic*] *Owd Bob*,[11] also Hilaire Belloc's *A Change in the Cabinet.*[12] So I am far from idle—and I don't intend to be again. I am enormously satisfied to have been able to tick these things off my list as 'things done' and am turning to other projects—I believe I will get all my ideas worked out in time, after all, or at least, most of them. whether they are worth anything or will secure publishers, Heaven only knows—I have shown Pavey much of my recent stuff, he being on the spot, and he enthuses. You and others have encouraged me before—anyhow the cacoethes scribendi[13] gives me no rest! I am not going to mention what I am turning my attention to now—I will tell you when and as the things get done. I only wish that circumstances were more accommodating and that you were nearer so that I could benefit by your advice as I go along—but in the meantime the thing to do (as I know now that I shall not get out of the Army for nearly a year yet!)[14] is to forge ahead and pile up completed stuff instead of listing intentions and dreams.

I am anxious to know how Kerr's book is getting on and wearying to see some of his stuff. I hope that he has now satisfactorily recovered from his wounds and has been demobilized.

I find time, too, I must tell you, for other things beyond writing and reading. How wonderful I am!! I was away all last week-end on special leave playing Rugby, as a wing three-quarter (Can you see me in that role?) for the Marseilles Base Team against a crack team of French aviators (who won by 8 points to nil after a swift bitterly-contested game) at the wonderful little Riviera resort of St. Raphael. I sustained gravelled knees, a split lip, and a priceless thirst, which I satisfied—headache in lieu. The match was on the Sunday—on the Monday another player and I went on to Cannes where we had an unforgettable six hours' medley-treat of white sun, blue sea, blossoming almonds and mimosa, glittering cafés, music and merriment. Thence back by the night express, running through an incomparable countryside doubly-magical under a sovereign moon, to Marseilles!

I am afraid this letter is scrawled even more atrociously than usual—my pencil is too slow. The alarming accounts in the papers of the amount of illness prevalent at home make me anxious that it may find you, and Mrs Ogilvie and the children, well. Exciting rumours of industrial happenings are trickling through[15]—I wonder what's what really, and, if there is to be anything really *big* doing, cannot imagine how I will support existence away here out of it all, at all, at all.

But I have already put more than a sufficient strain on your patience and powers of decipheration. I will write again soon. In the meantime I am longing for one of your letters once more. Please write soon.

With all good wishes,
I remain,
Yours Faithfully.
C M Grieve.

64020 Sgt C M G
RAMC
Sections Lahore Indian General Hsp, Marseilles.

NOTES

1   Hagar was the handmaid of Sarah and her stepson was Isaac, son of Sarah and Abraham. It is difficult to know what MacDiarmid means here.

2   MacDiarmid published 'Conrad: A Critical Estimate' in *Northern Review*, August 1924, p 240.

3   Leonard Arthur Pavey (1888–19?), British writer and journalist noted mainly for his short stories. Neither the sketch on Paris nor the work he was writing with Pavey were published. The verses were probably absorbed into work published at a later date, but the book on 'The Soviet State' did not appear and the manuscript has not come to light so far.

4   There is now no trace of this work.

5   Futurism was the artistic movement initiated by Filippo Tommaso Marinetti (1876–1944), an Italian dramatist, novelist, poet and critic who published mainly in French. His 'Manifeste de futurisme' appeared in the Paris *Figaro* on 20 February 1909 and the following year he gave lectures on Futurism in London. So called because they glorified youth, the future and mechanisation, the Futurists were advocates of non-representational art and influenced the development of Dadaism, Cubism and Surrealism.

6   Paul Valéry (1871–1945). Interested in Valéry's theories, MacDiarmid refers to them in several of his poems. *See also* his 'Rimbaud, Paul Valéry and others' (*The New Age*, 15 January 1925, pp 139–40) and 'Paul Valéry' (*The New Age*, 1 December 1929, p 54).

7   André Gide (1869–1951). Gide was, in 1909, co-founder of the *Nouvelle Revue Française* in which he published his own work and MacDiarmid may have been familiar with his writing from that source.

8   Albert Samain (1858–1900), French symbolist poet. The date of his death suggests perhaps that MacDiarmid's letters to these poets was more projected than prosecuted.

9   This work did not materialise, but several of MacDiarmid's contributions to *The New Age* deal with this topic.

10 George Moore (1852–1933), Irish novelist who introduced realism in imitation of Zola into English fiction. *Sister Teresa* (1901) is, however, a departure from his realistic style, having a strong theological element.

11 Alfred Ollivant (1874–1927), an English novelist whose dog story, *Owd Bob: The Grey Dog of Kenmuir,* was first published in America in 1898 where it became something of a cult. The book was later made into a film, *To the Victor,* which featured the Scottish actor Will Fyffe.

12 Hilaire Belloc (1870–1953). *A Change in the Cabinet* (1915).

13 The itch for scribbling.

14 After Armistice Day the government adopted a 'go-slow' policy towards demobilisation. The unemployment situation in Britain was getting steadily worse and fears were that if demoblisation took place too quickly it would result in a sudden and increased flood of the unemployed. In the face of what had happened in Russia and the industrial unrest that was taking place in Glasgow and Belfast, the government feared a civil crisis might be to hand.

15 In December 1918 John MacLean attempted to convert the Trades Council of Glasgow into a working Soviet. He had been arrested in April 1918 after his appointment by Lenin as the Soviet Consul in Glasgow, but was released after the war ended. Unemployment was rising rapidly both among the miners and in the centres of shipbuilding on Clydeside. Proposals were put forward by the Clyde Workers Committee to reduce the working week to thirty hours, a move which was seen as distributing what work there was more equitably. There followed a series of protest marches which culminated in a riot in George Square in Glasgow on 21 January 1919 at which the red flag was very much in evidence. The government, fearing that they could not rely on the loyalty of the police, deployed troops and armoured tanks into the centre of the city. Afterwards the leaders were imprisoned for 'incitement to riot', but the incident began a period of long and bitter industrial unrest throughout the centres of heavy industry and mining in Britain.

Post card with a view of Gavarnie—Le Cirque—L.L.

Villa de l'Annunciation, Lourdes

4 June 1919

Dear Mr Ogilvie:-

   You must excuse my slowness in writing you. I will write as soon as I get back to Marseilles—in a week's time. I have just returned from the Franco-Spanish frontier. This p.c. shows the great semi-circle of rock and snow dividing the two lands. Yesterday over fields of eternal snow I climbed right up the Brèche de Roland in Spain—about 3000 metres high—a wonderful experience. Tomorrow I am going on into Bryonne and Biarritz and thence into the Pays Basque and along the Silver Coast—Kindest regards to Mrs Ogilvie and the children. I hope this finds all well.

Yours.

Grieve.

PS   I expect to be home demobilized next month. Full details next letter.

S.L.I.G.H. Marseilles

12 June 1919

Dear Mr Ogilvie

Have just returned to find awaiting me yours of date 29/5/: and am hastening (happily) to accede to the little request you make therein in the hope that it may not be too late.[1] I am greatly interested in this idea of a Souvenir number and shall hope to be able to secure a copy. Probably however I shall see you before it is out, as I now find myself (rather unexpectedly) the next in this unit for demobilisation: which indeed may come through for me before the end of this week and at most cannot be delayed more than a fortnight or so.

I have unfortunately not got MSS here of Salonika Poems (or indeed of much else: as I have been sending stuff home for safe keeping or disposal otherwise practically as I wrote it)—nor can I rewrite more than one or two of them from memory. I enclose copy of one which you told me you liked.[2] If you remember any one which you would prefer to this one, please drop a note to Peggy at 35 South Street, St Andrews: and she will send a copy on right away. (I told you I had left the stuff with her to 'place' etc. but other matters have so occupied me lately that I have not even asked her to report progress and curiously enough she has not herself mentioned the matter.—However I'll be home soon now and [will] get things properly in train.)

I also enclose a set of verses I wrote on my Pyrennean holiday.[3] I wrote a great deal of various kinds but nothing else, I think, suitable for your purpose. But I rather like this little thing myself and perhaps it will fill a corner.

As to the sketch, this has me frankly beat. Looking over the stuff I have vainly and desperately asked 'Which?' Thinking over the material in my brain I have demanded 'What?' and 'How?' till I have tottered on the verge of cerebral vertigo. (Please do not construe this as indicating that your request has caused me any trouble!) Only one thing I have written has done, I think, any justice to my war experience and opinions—particularly opinions—but as it runs to about 200,000 words and is still in rough drafts, you will understand why I do not enclose it. But my month's demob leave is to be dedicated to its finishing.[4]—I think you will like it and perhaps find in it some little reward for your long faith in me.

Anyhow I have at last (with a sense of utter inadequacy) fixed on the enclosed sketch. I am sorry that I can do no better in the time at my disposal or under my present very unsettled circumstances.

You must please excuse too this quickly-scribbled letter. If I have time here I shall write again in a day or so and tell you of my wonderful time on the Spanish border—if not I will instead tell you of it by word of month: I am looking forward enormously to seeing you again shortly.

Many thanks for your kind remarks re Peggy. She has been a bit run down but is now on holiday down Selkirk[5] way.

My holiday did me a world of good. I don't remember ever feeling more fit. Kindest regards to Mrs Ogilvie and the children: and to yourself.

Faithfully,

Grieve.

PS   On second thoughts I'll send you another sketch tomorrow. Please use which you will.

[The above postscript has been cancelled out and while there is no manuscript attached to the letters in the collection, the sketch which follows appeared in *Broughton Magazine*, Summer 1919, pp 15–17.]

NOTES

1   Ogilvie had obviously asked for a written contribution from MacDiarmid for the Souvenir edition of *Broughton Magazine*.
2   Probably 'To a French Girl Friend' (*C.P.* II, p 1202) which was published together with the piece which follows in the Summer 1919 edition of the magazine.
3   One of which seems likely to have been 'Mountain Measure-Les Hautes Pyrenees, June 1919', (*C. P.* II, pp 1201–2).
4   *See* letter of 7 August 1919 where MacDiarmid states he has 'nearly completed' his '200,000' word 'novel'.
5   An ancient border town and popular tourist centre where the MacDiarmids spent several holidays.

CASUALTIES

For three weeks the working hours of the unit had been sixteen out of every twenty-four, and at length, in the centre of that sloppy and muddy field, appeared what was to be known to the Army as the Nth Casualty Clearing Station.

Tired enough from the strain of continued and unremitting road-making, tent-pitching, and the innumerable heart-breaking tasks incidental to the shifting of stoves and equipment, and the improvisation of those diversely essential things which cannot be secured except by indents which take many weeks to circulate through the chain of offices, the unit disposed itself, as units do, to snatch some sleep before the first rush should begin.

None too soon, it shortly appeared, for as we stumbled to the Fall-In, headlights began to appear on the road from Albert, a long trail of ambulance cars stretching back into the rainy dampness which hid the tremendous business so casually referred to as 'The Big Push'. The turn of the first car into the little road found a quietly active camp, for hasty preparations had been carried out in just such improbable corner-grounds many times before.

Here, as always in the track of armies in the Somme region, the salient element was mud—thick, deep, insistent and clinging mud that the strongest will could not treat as negligible. There it was and it made the smallest errand an exacting fatigue. The cars manoeuvred through it with the casual air that comes of much experience. Even London taxi-drivers might have learned something from the dexterous and undelaying way in which Red Cross cars were juggled over that boggy land. One by one the cases were slid out by stretcher-bearers working deftly and surely with a sort of tired ease. Car after car rolled up—just the price of 'strengthening the line and solidifying positions in the neighbourhood of —————,' as it would appear from the day's official report. Men of all units, tired, pale and dirty, were carried into the hut that a party of engineers had finished feverishly that very day. Their khaki barely showed through the encrusting mud save where it had been slit to rags to allow of temporary dressings being put on at Field Ambulances and First Aid Posts and now showing in curious patterns of white and red. Among them were some to whom this station would be something more than a wayside resting-place, men to whom the doctors up the line, working in dug-outs where immediate attention to all could not be given, had given a desperate last chance. They died on the way or slipped off without fuss in the Receiving Room, but one or two were pulled through by efforts and methods that would stagger civilian practice.

All night the slow heavy labour of stretcher-bearing went on. And great grey cars pulled up with loads of less seriously wounded who straggled brokenly into the room, muddied and shivering, hatless and coatless often, and with that complete apathy of look and bearing which tells of strain that has gone beyond endurance.

The detached onlooker might have found it moving enough, but here, fortunately, there were no detached onlookers. Lady friends, of the type we all know, were compelled to find stimulants for their sentiment somewhat farther down. But, here, a man who had been shovelling mud from the road during a back-breaking afternoon was now booking particulars of the arrivals. But some stared blankly through the interrogator, deaf and speechless, shaking and quivering, and that matter-of-fact fellow entered them as 'Shell-Shock.—No particulars available', and they were led off in that new world of theirs to a mattress, and ultimately who shall say to what strange and undesirable destiny.

The slightest cases walked or limped casually up to the keen deft-handed doctor and his alert assistants with the air of men to whom this was but one more incalculable phase of a business whose immensity made all impressions unseizable. To them, indeed, it had been overwhelming, and many of them were so youthful that one felt that the first instinct of their mothers, could they have seen them, would have been to reprove them for being out without overcoats on such a night!

The lashed rows of marquees that had been dignified by the name of 'wards' received these exhausted men on straw palliasses and blankets, and even, for serious cases, cot-beds. Casualty Clearing Stations belong not to any particular division but to an army, and therefore hither came representatives of most of the troops of an Army—Canadians, New Zealanders and South Africans, as well as famous British regiments and new raised battalions, and sick from locally quartered West Indians, Artillery, Engineers, and billeted troops. And there were men in mud-stained grey, stoical as our own, who somehow seemed mere ordinary men again and enemies no longer!

Serious cases speedily filled every available cot and an overflow lay around on stretchers. From all sides came the accustomed moaning for water and the close and heavy breathing of those past even moaning. A strapping sergeant of New Zealanders, gasping out his last unconscious moments, was the first to go. There was no more than time for a quick laying out (with the boot which was hanging so unnaturally to one side, the foot came off too, despite bandages). His transit must have been a desperate gamble from the start—a wrapping in a rough blanket with scrawled particulars attached, and the big fellow who had travelled so far to his fate was taken on a stretcher to the marquee that served as mortuary.

Many joined him that night. With these hopeless ones there was no time even to stop to watch by the ebbing life, so many bedside fights there were where a forlorn hope still remained. Work went on without respite, changeless save for the occasional sudden appearance of officers who would leave a few hasty directions for the special treatment of cases which had just left their hands in the operation theatre. Those worst hours before the dawn passed in hectic attendance—the tiredness of the body had perforce to be treated merely as a clogging dream—and the day-staff came to the relief of worn-out men.

The peaceful dawn-wind smote the workers as they stooped to pass through the low canvas doorways and the first faint flush of red showed behind a tree on a far ridge.

Up to that ridge wandered the indescribable waste of the countryside, trenched and pitted and ploughed until it had become a fantastic and nightmarish wilderness. On this dreary tract nothing remained of the gifts once showered by nature. But the grim legacies of man at war were countless—chaotic and half-buried heaps of his machinery, munitions and equipment, and the remains of his hasty meals. And he himself lay there, shattered in thousands, to give a lurking horror to a treacherous and violent surface of mud and slime and unlovely litter. The very weeds which might have graced the desolation refused such holding-ground.

Pale now beside the compelling splendour of the reddening day showed the yellow stabs of our guns, flashes that had lit the sky in the night watches, and only the long road, never varying, told that the unspeakable harvest on the Somme was still being gathered in.

C. M. Grieve

PART TWO

1919–1921

Biographical Summary

MacDiarmid was demobilised sometime between 12 June and 23 July 1919. He immediately joined his wife where she had been living in St Andrews and soon found work in nearby Montrose as a reporter with the *Montrose Review*. After a few months he left this job and moved to a private estate in Easter Ross to take up a teaching post.

On his return to Scotland MacDiarmid was bubbling over with plans and ideas for his own work and for the future direction of Scottish literature. Encouraged by Ogilvie, one of his first enterprises was to launch an anthology which would bring together the work of contemporary Scottish poets after the model set by the five volume *Georgian Poetry*.

MacDiarmid initiated the series by contacting a number of well-known Scottish literary figures—John Buchan, Neil Munro and the border poet, Will H Ogilvie—all of whom wrote very traditional verse, much of it in Scots. But he also included writers like Roderick Watson Kerr, Joseph Lee and John Ferguson, whose poems were distinctively modern, indeed the first two wrote starkly realistic war poetry. MacDiarmid's own contributions were not very exciting, it was work he had written during his army days and there was nothing very original about it.

In planning the Second Series of *Northern Numbers*, MacDiarmid wrote to Ogilvie that this collection would 'technically and otherwise mark a great advance on No. 1'. Here, the more traditional poets were less evident, but interestingly, there was a greater representation of work in Scots, poetry which showed that the vernacular was entering a new phase of development. None of MacDiarmid's own contributions were in Scots, but this work was markedly different. His 'Sonnets of the Highland Hills' reveal the kind of metaphysical themes which were to dominate so much of his work and his poems in *vers libre* highlight his growing concentration on technique, as well as a greater awareness of the potential of rhythm.

By the Third Series of *Northern Numbers* it is clear that MacDiarmid was prepared to pursue a more radical course, but by this stage he was already planning his *The Scottish Chapbook* and urging Ogilvie to rope in as many contributors as he could. At the same time as he was editing both works and writing most of the contributions for *The Scottish Chapbook*, he began to produce an enormous amount of journalism. By November 1922 he had contributed 'Scottish Literature and Home Rule' to the Scottish Home Rule Association newsheet and was publishing articles on several of the contributors to *Northern Numbers* in *The National Outlook*, as well as working on a series, 'Contemporary Scottish Studies'. These last articles are of prime importance, for it was in these that he began, in the midst of a great deal of controversy (evidenced from the correspondence his articles generated when they were published in the *Scottish Educational Journal*) to criticise, attack and reassess the course of Scottish literature.

Unsure of his literary ability, MacDiarmid continued to look to Ogilvie for support and approval, at times making impossible demands on the older man. Yet, while Ogilvie reprimanded MacDiarmid for his persistent claims upon him, he was obviously touched by the way in which the young poet regarded him as the lifeline of his spiritual world and Ogilvie continued to try to draw out what was creative in a temperament so clearly the antithesis of his own. MacDiarmid's own need to prove himself to Ogilvie shows in the manner in which he writes excitedly to tell him of his latest triumphs and plans. It was in this period that MacDiarmid finished writing his first prose work, *Annals of the Five Senses*. He was also trying to launch another periodical—*The Scottish Nation*—which was to be the northern counterpart of *The New Statesman*. He planned at least another half-a-dozen works, most of which were not executed or have vanished with the passage of time, and his poetic output began to burgeon. He was sending batches of his poems to Ogilvie, begging for his commentaries while trying to explain and explore the spiritual experiences that lay behind those which he felt were most meaningful to him.

The frantic activity of the letters which follow are a complete contrast to those of the slow and long drawn-out days of his army years. But much that had been fermenting in those years was now coming to maturity and finding tentative expression in MacDiarmid's literary experiments.

65 Market Street, St Andrews

23 July 1919

Dear Mr Ogilvie

I was unable to get to the concert after all, having had to come straight on here through news that my wife had taken suddenly ill—chill and a sort of nervous breakdown—much better now. I hope I did not cause great inconvenience to Mrs Ogilvie and yourself by not turning up on the Saturday. Please accept my apologies. Peggy will look forward eagerly to the pleasure of meeting Mrs Ogilvie again—at Kingsbarns perhaps. To Kerr also I owe apologies and, like myself, have lost his address.

Can you please manage to let him know that Foulis has jumped our way a treat over that selected verse idea[1] and that it is essential that I should have his selections (four or five if possible) at the earliest possible moment—and if you can get in touch with him, will you ask him to write me to above address so that I can send him on certain information he wants which he should have had ere this but for my misfortune with his address?

What a host of 'can you's'?—and there's one more. If Mr Stewart[2] has succeeded in enlisting Donald MacKenzie's[3] cooperation, his selections also I should have as quickly as can be.

It struck me after our talk that perhaps Eddie Albert[4] has some stuff, too, and would like to come in? It is immaterial whether the stuff has appeared elsewhere before or not. If it has I will, if I have the writers' permission, receive the publisher's or editor's consent to inclusion.

So far as the matter stands the following are definitely 'in':-

> T S Cairncross
> R W Kerr
> Joseph Lee[5]
> Myself

Also my hopes are to secure

> Donald MacKenzie
> John Ferguson
> Edward Albert

And I am in correspondence with John Buchan and Will Ogilvie.[6]

Please give my kindest regards to Mr Stewart: and accept for yourself, Mrs Ogilvie and the children the best wishes of Peggy and myself.

> Yours sincerely,
> C M Grieve.

NOTES

1 *Northern Numbers*, First Series, published by T N Foulis (Edinburgh and London)
   November 1920.
2 John Christie Stewart, then Classics Master at Broughton.
3 Donald A Mackenzie (1873–1936). An anthropologist and folklorist, he had collected
   a great deal of Gaelic folklore and literature. His works include *Elves and Heroes*
   (poems), *Scotland and Ancient Kingdom* (1930), *Scottish Folk-lore and Folk life* (1935). He
   contributed to *N.N.* 1. *See also* letter 25 May 1921?
4 Edward Albert was another former pupil of Ogilvie from Broughton. He too was to
   make his name as a writer but he did not contribute anything to the *N.N.* series.
5 Joseph Lee (1878–1949). MacDiarmid knew him from his army days. Selections from
   his published war verse—*Ballads of Battle* (Murray, 1916) and *Work-a-day Warriors*
   (Murray, 1917)— were included in *N.N.*
6 Will H Ogilvie (1869–1963), a popular poet from the Borders who wrote mainly
   nature poetry. Selections from his works—*Whaup o' the Rede* (1909), *The Land we
   Love* (1910) and *The Overlander* (1913)—were included in *N.N.*

65 Market St., St Andrews

7 August 1919

Dear Mr Ogilvie,

Since I have not yet heard from you in answer to my letter asking you to be
good enough to link me up on to Kerr, and if possible to rope in Albert, and to
ask Mr Stewart if he had succeeded in securing Donald MacKenzie, I have
regretted all the more that instead of hurrying desperately to catch (by the skin
of my teeth) that train I did not wait for the next: and take my opportunity of
talking things over with you.

I am anxious to know as soon as may be whether or not these three are really
coming in to this first volume of *Northern Numbers*: I shall be greatly disappointed
if they do not. If they are it is essential that I should have their selections by the
earliest possible post. I have received all the others now and they are already in
the hands of the publishers. These are:- John Buchan, Will H Ogilvie, John
Ferguson (author of the *Thyrea Sonnets*, now in their *sixth* edition—Ye Gods!),[1]
Thomas Scott Cairncross, and Joseph Lee, the author of *Ballads of Battle*. Also
mine.

And by permission the first volume is to be dedicated to Niel [*sic*] Munro.[2]
Please try to send me Kerr's address if you can.

Apart from all that I have now nearly completed the devastating task of writing out my novel— am on the very last lap—over 200,000 words.

Also other things of which more anon.

In our 'wee house' we have at present no fewer than three girl friends staying—I feel as if I were imprisoned in Girton.

You too will now be on holiday. I hope you are having a good time. Please give my kindest regards to Mrs Ogilvie and Agnes and John. And accept the same yourself. Peggy joins me in this.

Hoping to hear from you soon and to see you soon.

I am.

As Ever.

C. M. G.

NOTES

1   Ferguson's work was to go through a total of fifteen editions.
2   Neil Munro (1864–1930), popular Scottish novelist noted for his short stories and romances—*The Lost Pibroch* (1896), *John Splendid* (1898)—as well as his verse—*Bagpipe Ballads and other Poems* (1917).

65 Market St., St Andrews

10 August 1919

Dear Mr Ogilvie,

Glad to get your note of y'day's date. I expect that my trouble through the missing letter was really occasioned by my inveterate bad habit of sending letters to you to the J S Centre [Broughton Junior Student Centre]. I really must begin to keep an address book.

Yes. The first volume is to be entirely verse (with an intro, biographical short notes, and bibliographical notes where needed). The subsequent numbers will also be all verse, except where one or two suitable one-act plays may be procurable. Joseph Lee has promised to do something in that line. And I am hopeful of 'roping in' Eric Lyall.[1] Even then, however, not so much one-act plays as dramatic poems will be used.[2]

I shall be extremely glad if you do manage all right to get Albert to let us have one or two of his poems—5 is almost the run, if his section is to be proportionate to the others.

By special permission the volume is to be dedicated to Neil Munro. (I do not know if I mentioned that before.)

I do not know what to do about Donald Mackenzie: as of course I have not Mr Stewart's address: and after the holidays will be too late.

I shall be extremely glad to see you some day this week.

Please give Mrs O. and the children my kindest regards.

Yours.

Grieve.

NOTES

1 Eric Lyall did not contribute to any of the *N.N.* series.
2 Poetry, mainly short lyrics, was all that was published in *N.N.*

On 6 October 1920 MacDiarmid took up a post as teacher to the two daughters of the head stalker of Kildermorie Forest, located on a private estate near Alness which is a village ten miles north-east of Dingwall in Easter Ross. He was to remain there until 26 April 1921.

The letter which follows is undated, but as it was written from his new address it must have been sent sometime after 6 October 1920 and before the letter of 24 October 1920.

Kildermorie Forest Lodge,
Alness, Ross-shire.

[Early October 1920?]
Saturday

Dear Mr Ogilvie,

A lean week! Nothing of interest to report. My wife returned (after 5 weeks absence) on Thursday: and we are busy entrenching ourselves, in all the ways that one needs must at a distance of 17 miles from the nearest village, against the rigours to come—rigours already most unmistakeably adumbrated in a terrific and soul-freezing frost. Praise be it is luxuriously comfortable indoors—and I have barely five minutes walk to school.

'School', I should explain, is 2 pupils—girls—one Supplementary, one Standard V. The marriage of their former teacher and the practical impossibility of procuring another to sojourn in this fastness led to my being offered—and accepting—the appointment. I find it positively fascinating—which of course would not be the case under almost any other circumstances.

I apologise most unreservedly for setting up Wells as a scoring point.[1] My odious journalistic instinct often betrays me into ill-considered retorts. Au fond, I think I am fairly sound. I am however tremendously fond of arguing—often for arguing's sake—but I cannot argue really. Sometimes I think that I only think that I can think. It is difficult to know—and it doesn't matter.

I did apparently misunderstand certain of your criticisms. I thought that you were objecting to one sonnet embodying an eternal concept, and another prophesying oblivion. I sought to set up a defence for the duality of—shall I say—my desire in this matter: because, other differences aside, I do attach supreme importance to the fundamental thought or ethical content of all literary work. There would have been no argument if I had read your remarks as criticising a conflict or contrareity of view within the scope of a single sonnet—because there can be no two opinions on that. In the sonnet in question I think the line I substituted for

'O Wind of love blow cold upon Him then'

my

'O Force Creative fail within Him then'

disposed of the logician's objections and greatly strengthened the whole sonnet.[2]

I am tremendously relieved to know that my tortuous spirit did Mr Stewart the injustice of imagining an impossible reason for his delay in writing. I must endeavour to make up in some other way for this infirmity in my general disposition to amity.

Excuse this scribble. Perhaps by next week I may have matter of greater moment to exercise my pencil upon. If you are busy do not trouble to answer this note—wait till some communication of more consequence suggests a real need rather than my ordinary perpetual desire for a letter from you in reply.

With every good wish.

Yours faithfully,

C M Grieve.

NOTES

1   Unidentified.
2   The sonnet is 'Acme' from the 'Sonnets of the Highland Hills' sequence (*C.P.* II,
     p 1210).

Kildermorie Forest Lodge

24 October 1920

Dear Mr Ogilvie,

Will you not forgive me and write? Mr Stewart said that you would. But no letter has come.

You must have wondered how I was enjoying this. It has been the most unqualifiedly successful experience I have yet made in a life of ups and downs. I intend to remain here as long as circumstances will permit.

But neither what was, nor is,—still less what may be—must be the theme of this note. Mrs G. is holidaying and I am bird alone. So once again I have had to write poetry instead of living it.

A week ago it struck me that it would be an interesting exercise to write a volume of sonnets. Forthwith I planned a book to consist of a dedicatory sonnet, 4 sequences of 12 each, and a valedictory sonnet—50 in all. I have so far succeeded in writing (if they may be called sonnets) the 29 I enclose.[1] I account it a creditable week's work. The quality is of course unequal. The form is not one in which I shall ever feel at home. I do not attempt to defend sestets which are impermissable with the octaves chosen—still less to defend the varied quatrains in one of the octaves. But – – – –?

Please tell me!

Hoping that this note may find you in fine fettle, and with kind inquiries as to the health and happiness of Mrs Ogilvie and Agnes and John.

I remain,

As Ever.

Grieve.

NOTES

1   Published as 'Sonnets of the Highland Hills' in *N.N.* 2, they were accompanied by a
    note which stated, 'These five sonnets are taken from a privately-circulated sequence
    of fifty'. The titles of the five which appeared are, 'Courage', 'Heaven', 'Rivals',
    'The Wind-Bags' and 'Valedictory' (see *C.P.* II, pp 1205–8). A further series of
    'Sonnets of the Highland Hills' appeared in *The Scottish Chapbook* (November 1922)
    with the titles 'High Over Beauty', 'Within that Week', 'Eden Regained', 'Acme',
    'The Outer Night', 'Funeral' (see *C.P.* II, pp 1209–12). As far as can be determined,
    these are all that have survived of the original fifty.

Kildermorie Forest Lodge

2 November 1920

Dear Mr Ogilvie,

I apologise for having trespassed so flagrantly upon your scanty leisure. It was
characteristically thoughtless on my part not to have written first and asked
whether you would care to see my sonnets and express an opinion on them.
Much of the 'difficulty of my case' arises from the fact that au fond I am ill-bred.
The frigid fairness of your reply perhaps punished me sufficiently. I shall not so
presume again.

Your letter is however to a certain extent incomprehensible to me. For
instance you say 'you don't seem to worry very much about yourself—it is a
pity for your own sake, etc., that you don't keep a firmer hold upon yourself—I
don't know what your peculiar temptation is but it has had a good innings'. It
would have been truer to say that I worry about nothing else—I have worried
myself practically into insanity in the hopeless endeavour to realise the promise
some people found in me. I have kept a strangle-hold upon everything but my
imaging faculty. I live (as my wife can tell you) a life of constant discipline quite
abnormally rigorous. The Spartans were libertines in comparison. I am
mobilised to the last fraction of sentience to one end and one end only. My
'temptation' lies simply in the fact that when I recurrently reach a certain pitch
everything outside me ceases to exist. At Montrose,[1] despite this intense and
monopolising inner life I nevertheless discharged my duties so well that I earned
the esteem of all with whom I came into contact—so much so that when, to my
employer's disgust, I left (which I did simply and solely because although I was
flourishing financially and socially, I was not getting sufficient leisure for original
work, and consequently verging upon a breakdown) the almost blasphemously
ironical incident happened of my receiving from the Town Council a vote of
thanks for my eminent public services! My 'temptation' simply arises from the

fact that it is impossible to serve God and Mammon—and I have a wife and myself to keep.

You say that you will treat me as I treat you. Except in my difficulty in maintaining a correspondence (which I have tried hard to explain) and my incorrigibly maladroit terminology when I do write (which you can discount), how have I treated you? I have turned to you in every need with utter confidence. I have loved you above all men and women. You have been constantly in my thoughts. I have sought in season and out of season to justify the faith you expressed in me. Can you not imagine the terror it has been to me to hear your predictions as to my literary abilities? I scarcely ever put pen to paper without first re-reading all your letters—just to make sure that they were really addressed to me—that it was of me you said all these impossible things! Do you think I want money or position or reputation? No. Do you think that it matters to my wife, for instance? I may dedicate my poems to her but do you think she reads them? And if she did do you think she would understand them, or me? No! I need not write. I can dream my books and enjoy them in my head. But I try to write incessantly and cannot help doing so because your commendation of my work is my only desire. If my work gives you no pleasure—if my work does not satisfy you that you saw true away back in those Broughton days—it is wasted, irrespective of anything else. I own no duty, in connection with any power of expression I may have, to anyone. God and man may be, as they like. But for you I will do all that lies within my power. In the light of that, can you understand what it means to me, chaotic among my private tragedies and nourishing myself on this solitary flame, to have you write 'I have had no time to do more than glance at your sonnets'?

I wrote these sonnets under an urge of despair. If they are not good enough I shall try again and again. While your acute criticisms have been infinitely helpful to me in issues of detail, your reply did not tell me what I wanted to know. Did they *satisfy* you? Did they leave you with the same notion of my ability as before? And where do you place them? I wanted to know what relative position you thought they would if published procure for me among contemporary poets. I cannot determine for myself whether I am on the right lines or not.

For good or evil, beyond all turning back, I do regard myself, thanks to you, as dedicate and I will exhaust every endeavour as long as I live to win out on the highest level.

When I was a boy at school, my old Headmaster said to my ineffable disgust, 'If he is careful he will be another J M Barrie'[2]—probably the cause of my scrupulous carelessness in many respects!—and if today you can say no more—I am spending myself in vain ambitions—and my 'peculiar temptation' is to keep on so spending myself.

I will go far beyond the stage of fragments—I have piles and piles of MSS—but not until in every case I am assured in advance of the precise place each volume will take in its particular field and its worthwhileness in view of my single goal.

And there is nobody who can so assure me, nobody whose opinion is of the least consequence to me, but yourself – – and even you circumstances which I will not have altered debar me from consulting except on questions of literary merit.

Yours sincerely,

C M Grieve

NOTES

1   As a reporter with the *Montrose Review*.
2   James Matthew Barrie (1860–1937) b. Kirriemuir, Angus. Scottish novelist and dramatist whose 'kailyaird' novels were enormously popular in the 1890s, but who, together with other 'kailyairders' was to become the focus of MacDiarmid's attack on the old guard of Scottish culture. Novels—*A Window in Thrums* (1889), *The Little Minister* (1891). Dramas—*Quality Street* (1902), *The Admirable Crichton* (1902), *Peter Pan* (1904). See *C.S.S.*, pp 3–4.

Kildermorie Forest Lodge

13 November 1920

Dear Mr Ogilvie,

No! I do not believe in consistency. And I am not going to pretend that I attach any great importance to the merely reasonable. Oblivion and a life hereafter are complementary notions.[1] Both attract me: and I am prepared for either. Their attraction predominates alternately.

> "Grant it to come to me also to keep
> This small session in camp at end of day,
> To have this waking witness ere I sleep
> Of the world passed away;
> Whether dreams take me then, or heralds wait
> As singing waters children say;
> Or ushers of the stars, bewildering fate,
> Upon the walls of darkness: or not less
> To be desired than they
> Calmer forgetfulness!"[2]

– – – After all our powers of expression and perception are at best five dimensional: and the Universe – – –?

Nor do I admit that I will anywhere find a wiser or safer guide, philosopher and friend than you are. I have my own opinion of my work—and my own general literary ideas—wherewith to offset the opinions you pass. I agree that your fondness for me may corrupt your judgement. I make the necessary allowances. But I value and want; and in fact need and will not matter how far I go continue to need your opinion first and foremost—It enables me to regard the showers of rejection slips with equanimity!

I am standing before the Citadel of the Dark Denizen all right: and I have my slughorn ready: and my lungs are splendidly sound—but unfortunately I am in the clutches of two Policemen—Indifference and Preconceived Ideas—who are determined to prevent me making what they call a breach of the peace. I shall break out of their hands all right—but in the meantime their clutch is too tight.[3]

You must not imagine that I am devoting any material fraction of my time to building Spanish castles. My work is by no means all in the future. 'Cerebral and Other Studies' is in the hands of the publishers[4]—and is the first of a series of 10 volumes of short stories all of which are either absolutely finished or in complete draft—over 100 stories in all, which will complete my work in this region of, shall I say, mystical psychoanalysis.[5]

'The Road to Spain', a volume descriptive of a holiday in Les Hautes Pyrenees—with sections of verse—is also in the hands of the publishers.[6]

'In the Tents of Time' is a series of post-war essays, psychological in interest and concerned principally with the reactions to war experience of the imaging and expressing faculties. Contributors—Joseph Lee, L A Pavey, Kerr and self. My own essay is completed (15,000 words) and is being typed. All MSS are promised me by the end of this month. Buchan is to write an analytical introduction. Foulis is publishing in the Spring.[7]

I am also busy with a volume of Contemporary Scottish Writers[8]—R B Cunninghame Grahame,[9] [sic] Neil Munro, Buchan, etc. etc.—for Leonard Parsons' 'Contemporary Series'—and have promised the MSS not later than the first weeks of the year. Spring publication also.

Then articles of mine on Lee, Kerr, Cairncross, and Ferguson are appearing (starting this next week, I think) in the *National Outlook*.[10]

These are not intentions—but things actually done—written and accepted! And I think you will agree that they represent a fair amount of work when you take into consideration the fact that in addition to my other duties here I am local 'headmaster' under the Ross and Cromarty Education Authority and put in full school hours, and teach all the requisite subjects for Class V, and Supplementary!

I would willingly share with you the fun connected with my appointment here. It is the most incredible mixture of phantasy and reality: and (permit me my oblique little satisfactions) overwhelmingly impossible to any one less 'mixed' than myself. However I must ask you to wait a little longer—I have drafted a book entitled 'Oddman Out: Notes from a Highland Pantry'.[11] Once I can get a start on it I will write it in no time. I am sure that you will enjoy it. I should like to know what you did reply to Col Cuthbert[12]—who, by the way, is factor: my employer is C W Dyson-Perrins,[13] the Worcester Sauce multimillionaire and one of the most delightful and original little good-hearted freaks in Christendom!

But after all, although I get a chance to write here which I could not get in Montrose, I am not apparently to be permitted to enjoy my wilderness as long as I had hoped. I had hoped to remain here for a couple of years anyway—but do not be surprised if I am in Edinburgh for good in a few weeks' time. I have applied for a job—but just for a time if I do get it. I do not care much either way. The 'New Scotsman' is coming off![14] And I am just about 'snowed under' with preliminary correspondence and arrangements. It will be a very big thing. However as soon as matters are definitely fixed up and a date can be settled for launching out I will make an opportunity of seeing you and going as thoroughly into the matter with you as you have time for. What I feel I should really like and benefit by would be a thorough cross-examination into my theories of life, literature, politics and religion. I feel pretty sure of myself: but before taking on such a task I would like to 'mak' siccar'.[15] In the meantime I am doing a power of reading—I have accumulated big reserves of practicable journalistic ideas— and I am in constant correspondence with several prominent Scottish politicians and writers who have promised to support the venture.[16]

That is not all. Foulis has practically agreed to start a monthly (1/-)[1s. 0d.] *Scottish Chapbook* under my editorship—to set a national standard, to sort the grain from the chaff, to discover and encourage new Scottish poets, to move Towards a National Theatre etc. etc.[17] I just sent him my final proposals the other day and it is next to certain that he will decide to go forward immediately. Among the first contributors will be Lady Glenconner, [18] General Sir Ian Hamilton,[19] and Sir Ronald Ross.[20]

I do not want you to imagine that I am in any danger of dissipating my energies by tackling too much. Not so! I feel fully equal to a bigger programme than that: and much of the energy called for to carry through these schemes is old stuff I have had bottled up for this emergency for several years. What I mean is that I am not attempting in any way to start making bricks without having seen to it that I have ample stores of straw available.

An egotistic epistle! Reading between the lines will reveal easily enough the sort of man I am. The reason why I am anxious to limit our expressed relationships to what seem safe grounds of literary interest merely is that, while I am afraid that you might find closer intimacy disappointing—nay, quickly insupportable, I am in certain respects so definitely committed to courses of living (which I know you would not only not condone but could scarcely overlook—to your own sorrow, as I foresee, and increased anxiety, and finally perhaps, to a washing of your hands) that I am anxious to spare the few friends I do vehemently need to retain, the useless pain of endeavouring to help where I am unutterably determined not to be helped. I hope that despite the length of the sentence I have contrived to make myself clear.

At the same time I am touched to my very heart's heart by your letter and profoundly grateful to whatever Gods there may be to have such a friend. I shall not disappear again: and I shall write you, storm or shine psychologically, as regular as clockwork, every week-end in future so that you may at least always know where I am and what I am doing.

You will know however that there is at least one chamber in the heart of every real man to which he can admit no other—to which under certain circumstances he dare scarcely venture himself—and it is in that secret chamber that the most terrible encounters of a life which in any case never set much store by either material or spiritual happiness or peace must continue apparently without intermission to be fought. Which of course entails now and then such a participation of my external elements in the fray that I tumble before the incredulous eyes of one to whom I may be speaking into sudden and complete chaos—to all appearances!

Yours Ever.

C M Grieve.

PS   And whatever you do please do not imagine that I pity or indulge myself in any way.

NOTES

1   'The Wind-bags': '-And now converse, see-saws of sighs and groans,/Oblivion and Eternity together!' (*C.P.* II, p 1207)
2   These lines may have been written by MacDiarmid. 'Camp' in the second line suggests the period of the First World War; the cosmic imagery ('ushers of the stars', 'walls of darkness') is characteristic of his early poetry and the Eternity/Oblivion theme ('the world passed away', 'or heralds wait', 'Calmer forgetfulness') was obviously pre-occupying him.
3   A parody of Christian in John Bunyan's *Pilgrim's Progress*.
4   'Cerebral' is the title of one of the pieces of *Annals of the Five Senses* (1923). Foulis originally agreed to publish *Annals*, but when they were unable to do so, MacDiarmid published it himself.
5   MacDiarmid was to publish several of these in periodicals, although those that have survived fall far short of the original '100'. Kenneth Buthlay has collected some of these stories and published them together with other uncollected prose in *The Uncanny Scot: A Selection of Prose by Hugh MacDiarmid* (1968).
6   No work of that title was published and there is now no trace of the manuscript.
7   The archives of Foulis are not available, but Miles Marshall who was on the publishing side of the company after his father bought it in 1930-1, and who had a good knowledge of the early books, does not recall this work.

8 Published from June 1925 through to 1927 as 'Contemporary Scottish Studies' in the *Scottish Educational Journal*. A selection of these articles was published by Parsons in 1926 as *Contemporary Scottish Studies*.

9 Robert Bontine Cunninghame Graham (1852–1936). Scottish author, adventurer and politician. He was the first president of the Scottish Labour Party (1888) and first president of the Scottish National Party (1928). His literary reputation rests mainly on his essays and short stories: *Success* (1902), *Faith* (1909), *Hope* (1910), *Charity* (1912). His *Scottish Stories* (1914) contain one of his most celebrated tales—'Beattock for Moffat'.

10 The series 'Certain Newer Scottish Poets' began in *The National Outlook* on 12 December 1920. The first article was on T S Cairncross and in the next three issues articles on Kerr, John Ferguson and Joseph Lee appeared in that order.

11 No manuscript of that title or subject has been traced.

12 ?Col Thomas Wilkinson Cuthbert, Lt Col with the 4th (Ross Highland) Battalion, Seaforth Highlanders. Ogilvie had possibly been approached by him for a reference.

13 Charles William Dyson Perrins (1864–1958). A retired captain of the Highland Light Infantry, he also collected illuminated manuscripts and early woodcut books.

14 *The Scottish Nation*.

15 'make sure'.

16 MacDiarmid was in correspondence with Roland Eugene Muirhead (1868–1964) who was a leading member of the ILP and who had formed a new Scottish Home Rule Association in 1918. It was he who financed *The Scottish Nation*.

17 *The Scottish Chapbook* was to be the second and most important of MacDiarmid's early editorial ventures. It was to function as the organ of the emerging 'Scottish Renaissance' and in it MacDiarmid published his early poems in Scots.

18 Pamela Genevieve Adelaide Glenconner (Baroness). Scottish writer noted for her *The Sayings of the Children* (1918). She did not contribute to *S.C.*

19 General Sir Ian Hamilton (1853–1947). Scottish writer and soldier. He was a general in the Dardanelles campaign about which he wrote *Gallipoli Diary* (1920). *See* MacDiarmid's commentary on his work in *C.S.S.*, pp 25–8.

20 Sir Ronald Ross (1857–1932). Scottish physician and author. He discovered the parasite which causes malaria, for which he received the Nobel Prize for Medicine in 1902. He was the only Scottish poet to be included in *Georgian Poetry*. Poetry— *Philosophies* (1910), *Psychologies* (1919). Novels—*The Revels of Orsera* (1920). He contributed to both *N.N.* and *S.C.* See *C.S.S.*, pp 23–5.

Kildermorie Forest Lodge

15 November 1920

Dear Mr Ogilvie,

I have to thank you for your exceedingly helpful—really the word shd. be relieving—notes. The main reason for hurry is that my poetic output has run

away with me lately—including sonnets, over 120 poems in less than five weeks!
I want to get through with this phase as rapidly as possible—without sacrificing
anything if possible—in order to disengage my mind, and apply it elsewhere.

I am afraid that 'The Following Day' is even more of a mystery to me than to
you.[1] It came into my head just as it stands on paper. I was drying some dishes—
stopped, wrote it down in a few seconds—and went on drying dishes, not
however without feeling curiously shaken. I recognised quite impersonally the
latent power of the thing—I tried to develop it afterwards: but soon found that it
was impossible. the 'We' and 'I' in the Soldier's Song is easily put right—by
making 'a song a soldier sung' instead of 'the soldiers sung' in the first stanza.[2]—
Otherwise I shall just leave it. It is only a fragment of something infinitely bigger
which will happen to me one of these days—and, have no fear, the big thing will
be clear enough.

You must not think either that I am at the mercy of moods altogether. Things
like this happen. How I know not. But as a rule I work with definite and
perfectly controlled intention. And I detest obscurity just as much as you do. I
will be the last man to mystify for mystification's sake. J C Squire's[3] notes ran as
follows:- 'I *do* think it "worthy of perusal" but not publishable. (i.e. in *London
Mercury*). It would be difficult to explain why. Had you sent 10 poems instead of
1 I would probably put my finger on things. It isn't only that the soldier's song
doesn't ring quite true and isn't in a convincing metre' (with which I am in utter
disagreement) 'e.g. "But" as a single line might do in a slow-going ode but not
in a reckless chorus'.[4] My ear is faulty, I know—I am as you know tone-deaf in
music and that does affect my work:—but I am convinced that it should be the
other way about: ' . . . but there are things forced or not easy to understand. *But*
there seems to me what I can only call *guts* in the poem and you should certainly
stick to it and send us some more in the same vein. It is only a matter of finding
yourself.'

However, that's that.

I quite agree with your criticism of 'The Spanish Pro'.[5] I really wrote it
[a]round this quotation from Henri Barbusse:-[6]

> Peu à peu mes regards du jour
> S'habituent à votre tendresse . . .
> Je comprends l'indistinct amour
> Et le mystère de caress.
>
> Je vois votre coeur rayonnant
> Dans la candeur crépusculaire.
>
> A force de tranquillité
> Vous brillez comme auprès d'un cierge.
> Dans le soir de réalité
> Où vous êtes un peu de Vierge.

Since writing it too I have discovered this fine line of Victor Hugo's which I shall place above my 'Eden Regained'.

'Un instant d'amour rouvre l'Eden fermé'.[7]

I do not think that theologically you are in the best—shall I say—of modern company. Wells[8] and many others have pictured the Lonely God still continuing to discover Himself. If that conception is right—then it follows that there is quite room for little lapses and forgettings as well as developings of new attributes. I agree of course that the whole is greater than the part—and consequently have changed.

'O wind of love bow cold upon him then!'

to

'O Force Creative fail within Him then!'[9]

Your view of 'The Windbags' is just what I intended to convey.[10]

I quite recognise that Death is a matter of comparative indifference to Humanity. This indifference I cannot share. One year with love will always remain to me more desirable than any celestial eternity. Whatever the Hereafter may be Death is to my mind a definite and irreparable loss, more or less serious—but serious always.

I know you are busy. It is selfish of me to keep on thus. But it does me good to unburden myself: and I know the breadth of your shoulders.

As Ever.

C M Grieve.

PS   No. no! I invite the public to share my hopes and fears. I do not pretend to omniscience: nor don the prophet's mantle. Final philosophic attitude should not be sought in a first book of poems. I must be permitted my ups and downs. I do not wish to be regarded as a 'one-sided case'. The very fact that I have written them at all is proof of an underlying sense of the worthwhileness of everything— life and death, sorrow and joy, love and lust, hope and fear, Eternity and Oblivion. I do not claim to look at things from God's altitude—but from a human and therefore necessarily incomplete angle. The Ultimate Perspective may be all-inclusive—ours is not yet, nor likely to be. It is God's own point of view that He is neither young nor old—from the human point of view each day ages everything, and certain minutes superannuate him.

PS   The 'F.D.' [The Following Day] intrigues me more than anything I have yet written. Of course I may yet undergo the actual experience of which, this shadow, fell across my mind. Or, in the same way, a stanza I have not so far been given may yet come and throw all the others into perfect clarity.

By the way I am troubled about Mr Stewart. Some weeks ago I wrote him a long letter criticising (on his invitation) certain translations and original poems of his. He has not written again: and I am very much afraid that he may have taken offence. I do not know what sort of man he is, you see. I expressed my view of his work with utter honesty and of course expected that he could sufficiently depersonalize himself to accept my views in the spirit in which I gave them. I shall be very sorry if I have lost his friendship in this way—especially as I emphasized the complete irreliability [sic] of my critical apparatus and was at considerable pains to let him know that although my opinions were as they were I attached little importance to them and hoped he would attach less.

NOTES

1   Published in *Annals*. See *C.P.* I, pp 8–10.
2   Refers to line 8 of 'The Following Day'.
3   John Collings Squire (1884–1948), English poet, critic and editor who was closely associated with the Georgian poets. He became literary editor of *The New Statesman* in 1913 and editor in 1917. From 1919–34 he was editor of the *London Mercury*, a leading literary periodical. MacDiarmid had sent 'The Following Day' to him, but as the above indicates it was rejected, a fate which later poems were also to meet (*See* letter 26 September 1921). Although MacDiarmid's editorial work received coverage in *The London Mercury* his poems seem to have been too strong for Squire's taste and were never published there.
4   Refers to line 19 of 'The Following Day'.
5   'Spanish Girl'?, also published in *Annals*. See *C.P.* I, pp. 10–13.
6   Henri Barbusse (1873–1935), French novelist and poet whose *Le Feu* (1916) was a powerful and realistic record of the war. He was associated with the Symbolist circle. The quotation is from his 'Apothéose' in *Pleureuses* (1895). In the original the last line reads, 'un peu la Vierge'.
7   Victor Hugo (1802–85). The quotation is from 'Les Trônes d'Orient—Sultan Mourad' in *La Légende des Siècles* (1859) and the original reads 'Un seul instant d'amour rouvre l'Eden fermé'.
8   H G Wells. A reference to MacDiarmid's interest in the representation of a God of process which Wells in his 'theological' novels—*Mr. Britling Sees it Through* (1916), *God the Invisible King* (1917) and *The Undying Fire* (1919)—had been exploring. Similarly, James Stephens, whose poem, 'The Lonely God', appeared in the first series of *Georgian Poetry*.
9   The line is from 'Acme', (*C.P.* II, p 1210). *See also* letter October 1920?
10 See *C.P.* II, p 1207 where its title is 'The Wind-bags'.

Kildermorie Forest Lodge

25 November 1920

Dear Mr Ogilvie

I have just received your note—dated *29th*, which more than eloquently speaks of worry—and I am just scribbling off this hurried response to let you know that I shall leave no stone unturned to secure you the necessary maid-servant.

As a matter of fact I know a girl who I am confident will suit you capitally. She is vacating her present service in a week's time. Her intention is to go home for a little and then seek another post. I shall have a talk to her tomorrow and am in hopes that I may be able to secure her for you.

If not, I can cast a pretty wide net here—I know heaps of servants of all degrees—and it will be strange if I can[not] get one of the number to realise the immediate attractions Edinburgh has to offer.

But the one I mention I shall be after to-morrow—because I know her for a good girl, a hard worker, and a 'stayer'.

Excuse brevity and wild pencilling. Had long letter from Mr Stewart. Other matters must be deferred to Saturday's letter—the post awaits.

Yours.

Grieve.

Kildermorie Forest Lodge

30 November 1920

Dear Mr Ogilvie,

Just time to dash off the smallest of follow-up notes to let you know that I have spoken to the girl I indicated; that she is leaving her present employment on Thursday; and that she thinks she would like to try Edinburgh all right but must mention the matter to her mother first whereafter she will immediately write me.

I think it likely that a solution to your difficulty will be found in this girl. At any rate I shall [a]wait her letter before trying elsewhere.

But if after all she decides not to consider Edinburgh: then I shall not lose further time in trying for other another (that sounds wrongly put—but I haven't time to reread it).

Excuse this indecent haste.

Yours Ever.

C M Grieve.

Kildermorie Forest Lodge

19 December 1920

Dear Mr Ogilvie,

I have been reluctant to write to you again until I could report definitely upon the Quest of the Golden Girl.

The girl of whom I wrote has after all decided that she must stay at home over the winter—her mother being far from well—but I have asked her to write me first when she thinks of taking another place.

Mrs G. is on the track of several other girls. I may have better news for you by any post. Of course one of the troubles is that any girl disengaged just now will want to stay at home over Christmas and the New Year.

But the quest goes on until the treasure is ours, one way or another.

You saw *N.N.* before I did. It was good of you to write so quickly.

It is selling splendidly. Reviews are not yet to hand—although I have just learned it was reviewed in the *Dispatch*, 16th.[1]

A special article on it will appear in next issue of *Scottish Field*.[2]

Impressions are everywhere wonderfully favourable. I have had a lot of most encouraging letters.

You prophesized aright. My circle is widening with a vengeance. I cannot keep ahead of my correspondence these days at all.

And I am choc-a-bloc in other directions. I have just arranged with Professor Gollancz[3] to write a book on 'The Future of Scotland' for the new 'World of Today' Series (Oxford University Press).

I am getting on well with my book on 'Contemp. Scot. Writers' for Parsons.

I shall be in Edinr. just after the New Year—perhaps for almost a week. I have some 'devilling' to do on George IV Bridge.[4] Also arrangements are being made for a dinner or something of that sort in connection with the *N.N.* group, most of whom have promised to be present. More as to that anon.

I owe Mr Stewart a letter: but can't find a moment yet.

Excuse the brevity of this letter. I did not write because I was eager not to have to disappoint you—I write now because I know how anxious you must be for news.

Hoping to have better tidings next time.

Yours,

Grieve.

PS   The other Grieve was my brother.—Did you not once meet him?[5]

NOTES

1   Reviewed in the *Edinburgh Evening Dispatch*, 15 December 1920, p 7. The review was favourable, describing the volume as 'a miniature academy of Scottish verse'.
2   No article on *N.N.* 1 appeared in this periodical.
3   Victor Gollancz (1893–1967), publisher, author and philanthropist. Founder in 1936 of the influential the Left Book Club. The book discussed was never published by Oxford University Press but in 1927 MacDiarmid published a work of a similar title, *Albyn, or Scotland and the Future* for Kegan Paul's Today and Tomorrow Series (*see* letter 30 January 1928).
4   The location of both Edinburgh Public Reference Library and the National Library of Scotland.
5   Andrew Graham Grieve contributed two poems to *N.N.* 1, hence Ogilvie's enquiry.

Kilermorie Forest Lodge

26 December 1920

Dear Mr Ogilvie,

I shall certainly forego the keenest delight life can have in store for me if I do not achieve, in time, such a reputation as will enable you to put all that you have thought and dreamt of me into black and white.

'C M Grieve: The Man and His Work' by Geo. Ogilvie will certainly be a book worthy living the most difficult of lives for. – – – – You obliterate my fears and all those disagreeable concomitants of a general uncertainty which spring from practical considerations of such matters as the perversity of publishers, the price of paper, etc.—so that I, too, share your desire that it were two years hence and my position secured.

Your all-too-generous article in the *B.M.*[1] has purged me, I think, of my last hesitancies and doubts. I have been reinforced with some of the exuberance I lost when I left Broughton. Almost I fancy that you have enabled me to recapture some at least of my old careless rapture. Certainly my pen is acquiring speed. MSS accumulate. Just as I owe the inception of the *N.N.* idea to you, so now I am indebted to you for a fillip to the sales I am sure. These debts—can I ever succeed in putting something really substantial on the other side of such a balanceless account?

Why, I have so far even failed in such a matter as procuring a maid. Another likely covert has just yielded a most disappointing blank. I could not have celebrated Christmas more happily than by succeeding in this quest. – – – I hope however that the third time will be lucky. In any case I shall not cease to do my utmost until either I succeed or you obtain otherwise the necessary girl.

My thanks for [the] *Scotsman* par:[2] I wonder if you could look out any day this week for a letter from me in *Scotsman* correspondence.[3] There may also be other letters before the end of the week. My methods in such matters are my own: and resemble those of the Heathen Chinee.

I shall certainly send on all reviews. Enclosed is quite a good one from the *Dispatch.*[4] The '—and Shadows' part of the title refers to subsequent paragraphs, unconnected with our book, but dealing with Murray's protest against unhealthy literature. The editor of the *Scottish Field* is having a special article on *N.N.*[5] It should be good. He's a good man—Brown, they call him.

He wrote re my article on Cairncross in December *National Outlook*[6]—'It is a piece of grand work which makes me envious'. The editor of the *Irish Times*[7] also wrote in flattering terms of its merit as journalism. Other tributes re this article were surprisingly enthusiastic—and unanimous. And I wrote down to the level of the paper! Honestly I did. The thing astounds me. Did you see it? I haven't a copy—but I can get you one. My article on Kerr appears in the January issue. It is published on the 15th of each month—3 Frederick St. Edinr.

Your final sentence stirs me as nothing else could. You say that you almost feel like writing yourself. I wish you would. Nothing has made me during these years lose whatever sureness of myself has occasionaly been mine than my periodical reflection on the receipt of letters from you that I was confirmed in my unfaith in the utility of literary endeavour by your contentment with the fallow-lying of gifts so immeasurably greater than mine.

You may be sure of me. I am infinitely more sure of you. And I know that whatever I may do will be a small achievement in comparison with what (for excellent reasons into which I shall never probe) you have deemed it best to leave undone.

I shall write you again as soon as I know definitely when I shall be in Edinburgh and when and where the dinner is to be.

Accept my assurance (as one who inter alia has written on 'Scientific Management' and 'Publicity and Propaganda Methods' in the *Advertisers'*

Weekly)[8] that I am alive to the fact that I have secured in you at any rate an incomparable press-agent: and have quite fallen in love again with the boy I used to be, as you picture the Then Me.

With best wishes to yourself and to Mrs Ogilvie and the children—in which Mrs G joins me.

Yours,

Grieve

NOTES

1   Ogilvie had written an article on MacDiarmid for the school magazine (*Broughton Magazine, Christmas* 1920, pp 9–13) in which he recalled his impressions of MacDiarmid at Broughton.

2   Ogilvie was perhaps instrumental in having *N.N.* 1 reviewed in the *Scotsman* (20 December 1920, p 2). The review praised the project and stated that it was 'an experiment in the publication of "group poetry", illustrative of the leading tendencies in contemporary Scottish verse. . . .'

3   MacDiarmid's reply to the reviewer appeared on 31 December 1920, p 2. He stated that the intent of *N.N.* was to set new standards.

4   The review of 15 December 1920 (referred to in letter 19 December 1920), the title of which was 'Northern Lights—and Shadows'. The first half of the title referred to *N.N.* while the second was a reference to a campaign launched by a publisher, John Murray, against sensationalism in literature.

5   The editor is unidentified.

6   'Certain Newer Scottish Poets: T S Cairncross' in *The National Outlook*, 12 December 1920.

7   ?Robert Maire Smyllie (1894–1954). Then assistant editor of the *Irish Times*. Born in Glasgow but brought up and educated in Sligo he was noted for his encouragement of new writers.

8   ?*The North British Commercial and Literary Advertiser*, published in Edinburgh during this period.

Kilermorie Forest Lodge

26 January 1921

Dear Mr Ogilvie,

I enclose herewith a few cuttings. I have others somewhere but can't lay my hands upon them at the moment—particularly a column one in *Glasgow Evening News* and my column-long reply thereto.[1] But these may interest and amuse you in the meantime. There are quite a number still to come in: also certain special articles based on *N.N.* I'll send them on as they come to hand. Who the 'W. J.' of the *Glasgow Bulletin* is I do not know?[2] I shall be glad if you can return them in a few days' time, as they are travelling round.

No luck yet in my search for a girl. I would not have believed so simple a commission could have proved so impossible to discharge. Fortunately—or rather unfortunately—your own experience will enable you to understand the reasons for 'this thusness' better than I do. I am told that a letter to the official in charge of the *Inverness* Labour Exchange would secure applications all right. Unemployment is rife there: and perhaps a good girl might be secured in that way, although it is not so satisfactory as knowing a girl would be.

I am busy now making arrangements for the second series of *N.N.*[3] I will let you know who the contributors will be—and in what proportions—as soon as I get matters fixed up.

I am also making headway with a volume of vers libre[4]—all on Scottish subjects, such as Edinburgh,[5] the Black Watch Barracks,[6] the Cowcaddens,[7] Verhaeren in Glasgow,[8] etc. I believe I will be able to place this all right. Some of it is humorous, as enclosed example[9]—least I think it humorous! A mixture of parody and passion!

I had hoped to be in Edinbr. ere this, but flu' broke out here. Mrs G had a bad time. I escaped rather easily. But that, and the fact that it prevented my getting on with my 'timetable' as I should otherwise have done, rendered a jaunt South out of the question. To my great disappointment I have no option but to adjourn my prospect of a break 'sine die'.

I am wading through quotations for the 'New Scotsman'. I am afraid that it is commercially out of the question to float such a paper in the immediate future—would cost over £20,000 per annum. But we'll see. – – I'll write soon again; Hope all well.

Yours Ever.

Grieve.

NOTES

1 An unsigned review of *N.N.* appeared in the *Glasgow Evening News* on 23 December 1920, which questioned it as a 'group' project and criticised the placing of established poets with 'a number of young poets of . . . questionable promise'. MacDiarmid's reply was published on 6 January 1921, p 2. He wrote, 'The contributors to *Northern Numbers* were a group only in the sense that they agreed to associate themselves with the same book. Beyond that, and beyond nationality and contemporaneity, they had obviously nothing in common. I have yet to see a homogeneous group of writers.'

2   William Jeffrey (1896–1946) who was then on the editorial staff of the *Glasgow Evening Times*. A journalist and poet, Jeffrey had just published his *Prometheus Returns* (1921) which MacDiarmid was to review in 'Scottish Books and Bookmen' in the *Dunfermline Press*, 11 February 1922, p 6. Jeffrey reviewed *N.N.* 1 in an article, 'Scottish Poetry: Is a Renaissance Taking Place?' in the *Glasgow Bulletin*, 17 January 1921. The modern temper of his poetry attracted MacDiarmid and his work was included in *N.N.* 3. *See also* MacDiarmid's article on him in *C.S.S.*, pp 43–5. Jeffrey's *Selected Poems*, edited by Alexander Scott, was published in 1951.

3   Published by Foulis in October 1921.

4   No volume was ever published separately, but one of the interesting differences between MacDiarmid's contributions to *N.N.* 1 and 2 is that in the latter he contributes poems which are in *vers libre*.

5   'Edinburgh' was included in *N.N.* 2. See *C.P.* II, p 1204.

6   A Scottish Infantry Division whose barracks were located in Glasgow. There is no poem dealing with that subject which has survived.

7   A slum district in Glasgow, again there is no poem of that title.

8   Emile Verhaeren (1855–1916). Belgian poet who was associated with the French Symbolistes. He wrote in *vers libre*, often about industrial landscapes, which is perhaps why MacDiarmid is associating him here with Glasgow. No poem of that subject survives.

9   There is no accompanying poem.

Kildermorie Forest Lodge

8 February 1921

Dear Mr Ogilvie,

I have always meant to dedicate to you something really good if—and as soon as—I could. This is not it. I have put your name above it and am sending it to you simply because you are the subject of it and were in my mind to the exclusion of all else when I wrote it.[1]

Please return it sometime in one of your letters. I haven't a copy: and am too lazy just now to make one. I have, as a matter of fact, had a bad turn—one of the worst since I came back. I took it in time. The diathesis of a severe relapse was there—but I managed, by dint of going to bed and staying there for a day or two, to prevent the development in it of the conditions of malaria and jaundice which threatened. I am however far from right: and must perforce ca' canny.[2]

Progress is being made with the arrangements for the Second Series of *N.N.* Most of the contributors—if not all: I have not yet heard from three of them—are appearing again: and all are out to make a Second Series which will technically and otherwise mark a great advance on No. 1. Sir Ronald Ross is joining us.

I have lost Albert's address again. Can you please give it to me? I am anxious to have him this time if he will come in. Have you seen any recent work of his?

I am anxious to know whether you are still without the girl. I can think of no avenue I have not explored, still open to me. And I am truly sorry. I would give a great deal to have been able to do you this small service.

I hope you, and Mrs Ogilvie and the children, keep well. All sorts of troubles seem to be going. Even up here we have had quite an abominable assortment.

I expect you are very busy.

Excuse this scrawl. All good wishes.

Yours as ever,

Grieve.

NOTES

1 'A Moment in Eternity' (*C.P.* I, pp 4–10). The poem was included in *Annals*.
2 'Be careful'.

Kildermorie Forest Lodge

22 February 1921

Dear Mr Ogilvie,

Excuse a short scrawl! I am keeping better but not quite myself yet. It is becoming intensely cold here. Spring does not whisper in these latitudes—she roars like a fish-wife.

I was surprised and delighted to find that you thought so much of 'A Moment'. 'Blind' is a word that means something to me quite unlike its normal or proper meaning—to me it is the antithesis of 'blazing', i.e. a steady light. cf. Rupert Brooke's

> 'The unnameable sightless white
> That lies behind the eyes.'

However I have altered it. I agree particularly with your pencilled suggestion of 'judgement' in lieu of 'criticism'. Judgement is *the* word.[1]

A special review of *N.N.* is to appear in the *London Mercury*[2] shortly—so the editor (Mr J C Squire) tells me in a letter to hand today. Squire seems to expect me to do things yet. *N.N.* he says still keeps him to his view that I haven't quite found myself yet—but he repeats all he said as to my promise.

General Sir Ian Hamilton[3] is joining us in the next series of *N.N.*

I am worried about Kerr. He sent me two pieces of deplorable stuff. I enclose these. Please return them. I should not perhaps send them without K's permission—but I want your help in dealing with him for his own good.

Kerr, however, also sent me the enclosed 'Ballad' by a young Edinr. fellow— an architect's clerk, called Wm Ogilvie.[4]

I should be grateful for your opinion of its merits. I think it is extraordinarily good. I have however edited it here and there,—mainly by entirely omitting two very weak verses.

I am looking forward to receiving your suggestions as to 'A Moment'. By the way, did you get the letter containing the poem on 'Edinburgh' and the jeu-d'ésprit, 'Playmates'?[5]

I hope this finds you recovered again: and Mrs Ogilvie and the children also well.

Best regards from Mrs Grieve and myself.

Yours Ever.

Grieve.

NOTES

1 MacDiarmid misquotes the lines from Rupert Brooke's 'The Fish' (published in *Georgian Poetry: 1911–12)*: 'And gold that lies behind the eyes,/The unknown unnameable sightless white/That is the essential flame of night'. 'Blind' refers to the line in 'A Moment in Eternity', 'Blind in the Godhead' and 'Judgement' to the line, 'Flame of creative judgement'. Part of Brooke's poem is also quoted in the opening of 'A Four Years' Harvest'.

2 *N.N.* 2 was reviewed in *The London Mercury*, February 1922, pp 428–9. The unsigned article praises the volume and singles out as 'interesting' Grieve's 'sonnets on hills' and the dialect poems of Charles Murray and Mary Symons.

3 Contributed to *N.N.* 2.

4 William Ogilvie (1891–1939). Scots poet whose work in the dialect was included in *N.N.* 2. He later published a selection of his verse under the title *The Witch* (1923).

5 Published in *N.N.* 2. See *C.P.* II, p 1204.

This letter is misdated. The references both to *N.N.* 2 and the poems 'Edinburgh' and 'Playmates' suggest that it would follow directly after letter of 22 February 1921. The probable date is 25 March 1921.

Kildermorie Forest Lodge

25 March 1919 [1921?]

Dear Mr Ogilvie,

I was concerned to learn of your continued indisposition. The thought of you ill powerfully dismays me. Your holidays will have begun. Wherever you spend them I hope you will have a splendid recuperative time: and that the Spring will oust whatever sickness may be in your veins. But alas! there is so much strange trouble abroad—one is anxious. I, too, am feeling far from well. My last touch of malaria has left me singularly weak and jaundiced. I would give a great deal for a sensation of vim.

I am agog with all manner of ideas: but my cerebrations are too enfeebled to clutch the winged things soaring incessantly just out of reach. Rather than be idle, however—and, of course, I do not believe in merely doing my best under the circumstances, but prefer to wait until circumstances are more favourable for seizing all that is still troubling me with its apparent unseizability—I have occupied myself with the more mechanical work of trying to make good to some little extent my deficiencies in the departments of the epigram and the short poem.

I have not succeeded in adding anything of moment to my little store of either: but I do not think what I have done is altogether wasted labour. I enclose a few examples, and will be glad to have your opinion. I was glad you liked the poem on Edinburgh: also the jeu d'ésprit 'Playmates' and thank you for your suggestions on both.

Mackenzie is a nuisance.[1] I have as a matter of fact gone a long way out of my usual to placate and propitiate him. He has given me more trouble—over nothing!—than all my other correspondents put together. His grouch originated from the fact that in the first volume of *N.N.* he was relegated to the back of the book—instead of figuring alongside the 'bigger men'! As a matter of fact I shirked my duty as editor: I did not arrange the order of contributors: but left it to Foulis. To save any similar dispute this time I am arranging contributors in alphabetical order. Mackenzie's all right—seems quite a decent sort of chap— except in re his own poems. Egotism I understand and like: but egotism that is camouflaged as disinterested advice—the sunflower masquerading as the violet— I detest. As far as I am concerned I do not care if M's contributions are given first place—but if they were I should have all the other contributors rearing up. M. is not popular in any case: and he is to my mind in every way a smaller man than Ferguson, Lee, and one or two others.

But I am confident that if Mr Stewart or you were to read my letters to him (having read his to me) you will acquit me on any charge of want of tact: and see me in a peculiar light as a monument of superfluous patience.

Enough! As a matter of fact I do now understand so well the petty troubles and difficulties of literary work that I wholeheartedly sympathise with every foible, however preposterous, of every scribbler, however small:—a sympathy that is, alas! complicated and in certain cases nullified in exact proportion to the number of correspondents to whom I must simultaneously extend it.

With best wishes and renewed thanks,

Yours Ever.

C M Grieve.

NOTES

1   Donald A MacKenzie. He was later to attack MacDiarmid's plan for a Scots revival. *See* his letter in *Scottish Educational Journal*, 9 October 1925, p 1105 and MacDiarmid's reply to it, 16 October 1925, p 1133.

The manuscripts which follow were included with this letter. 'Withered Wreaths' appeared in *N.N.* 2 and *Annals of the Five Senses* as 'The Last Song'. 'A Fool' appears in *Annals* as 'The Fool'. These poems were collected and published by J K Annand as *Early Lyrics* (Akros) 1968.

Ennui

I hear what the bird sings
(Cuckoo! Spring comes in!)
And know what the bell saith
(Ding! Dong! The worms win!)
And tire but of two things
—Life and Death!

A Fool

He said that he was God.
'We are well met', I cried,
'I've always hoped I should
Meet God before I died.'

I slew him then and cast
His corpse into a pool.
—But how I wish he had
Indeed been God, the fool!

She Whom I love

She whom I love hath many eyes
Since with the waters and the skies
She watcheth me: and openeth
Light after light within my heart
Naught in my secret dreams hath part
Save 'It is good' she saith
With a clear eye
That shineth by.

Withered Wreaths

The Heavens[1] are lying like wreaths
Of dead flowers breaking to dust
Round the broken column of Time.

Life a fitful wind and a cold
That rustles the withered stars
And the wisps of space is my rhyme,[2]

Like a fiftul wind and ~~colder~~ a cold
That whistles awhile and fails
Round the broken column of Time.

Tryst in the Forest

With starry eyes she comes to me
Between the dim trees there.
Love is the rosebud at her heart[3]
And Time the ribbon in her hair.

On cloudcool breasts she'll cradle me
In the long darkness there
With Dust the rosebud at her heart[4]
And Death the ribbon in her hair.

Truth

Lo! Youth!
In the heart of the world
Like a knife
Quivers this truth.
All that lacks love
Lacks life!

Two Gods

'The present moment is a powerful Deity'—*Goethe*

Now is a might God,
Then an unknown.
The One shall have my heart,
The Other own
The dreams I dare
Not let my own heart share.

In Memory

Only the rosebud I remember
Only the rosebud and the one green leaf
And lest these fail me too I make
The little summers of my spirit brief.

Only the rosebud I remember:
Only the rosebud and the one green leaf
My fearful breast to breasts of dust
Restores between the winters of my grief.

Only the rosebud I remember,
Only the rosebud and the one green leaf
—Beneath the gravestone of the sky
At last I lay them—a sufficient sheaf!

To Margaret

As from a hedge
Wild roses do
So from my dreams
Spring dreams of you.

And thoughts of you
In my thoughts are
As twixt dark clouds
A thrilling star.

1 Not capitalised in published version.
2 Reads 'And the wisps of space is my song' in the published version.
3 Reads 'Love is the rosebud at her breast' in the published version.
4 Reads 'With dust the rosebud at her breast' in the published version.

PART THREE

1921–1923

Biographical Summary

MacDiarmid resigned from his post as teacher at Kildermorie on 26 April 1921. He then returned to Montrose to work once again as a reporter with the *Montrose Review* and was to remain in that job (despite attempts to find other employment) for the next eight years.

The relationship between MacDiarmid and Ogilvie began again to show signs of strain in this period, but in general Ogilvie continued to give his support and encouragement. In addition to the later series of *Northern Numbers*, *The Scottish Chapbook* and *The Scottish Nation*, MacDiarmid was also editing the *Northern Review*, another ambitious journalistic enterprise dedicated to literary devolution which enlisted the help of 'Newcastle, Manchester and Liverpool' in its aims of breaking the hold of 'cultural centralisation in London'.

His literary output continued apace and there are references to novels, short stories, sonnet sequences, and so on. The poetry in English was becoming increasingly individualistic, as the two poems he sent to Ogilvie—'The Universal Man' and 'Cattle Show'—demonstrate, but MacDiarmid was frustrated by the fact that try as he may he could not get any of his work published in English literary journals.

The first letter from Montrose is undated but must have been written sometime betwen 26 April 1921, when he left Kildermorie, and 8 September 1921, the date of the letter which follows. Little correspondence seems to have passed between the two men in the intervening time because MacDiarmid refers specifically to the lapse in their letter writing.

19 Kincardine Street, Montrose.

[September 1921?]

Dear Mr Ogilvie,

I will write you fully in a few days—on Thursday perhaps. I shall be tremendously busy till then. This intermittent aboulia which renders me impotent to maintain regular relations with people has been extraordinarily well-developed this time. It has been physically impossible to write. However I objected strongly to passing out into the void again—and some time ago I shall [*sic*] [asked] my mother who is in Edinburgh to call upon you and explain why I wasn't writing. It is a terrible business and developed quite unexpectedly.

I have however been writing a great deal all this time. The *Northern Numbers* volume is all right—but for typographical reasons publication has had to be postponed till early in the Spring.[1] I have heaps of things to tell you and show you—mainly short stories. But I am making no effort to place them—all I feel interested in is to write them.

I was sorry to hear illness had spoiled your holiday: and hope you are completely rid of the trouble.

My own health is very shaky. The cold weather is playing me up in all sorts of unpleasant ways.

However, I'll write fully on Thursday.

Please forgive me.

C. M. G.

NOTES

1   *N.N.* 2 was in fact published in October 1921.

12 White's Place. Montrose.

8 September 1921

Dear Mr Ogilvie,

I am sending you herewith a set of the proofs of my forthcoming book,[1] which I think you will like to see. There are many mistakes as you will see: but these I have all corrected already: and the book will be out very shortly now.

So will the Second Series of *N.N.*, proofs of which I am now passing through.

I am sorry that neither of these volumes contains any poems of mine new to you: but I sent off on Tuesday last a set of seventy new ones—all, nearly, songs and little lyrics, written during two week-ends—to Andrew Melrose, publisher, who, I have reason to hope, will issue them under the title of 'Shapes and Shadows' this season yet.[2]

I had hoped to have seen you in Edinburgh ere this: but may do so soon. I hope you are keeping well—also Mrs Ogilvie and the children. Mrs Grieve joins me in sending our best regards to all.

As to other matters this kettle may have been exceptionally long in coming to the boil—a waited-on kettle has always a well in it however—but it is singing quite promisingly now.

With all love.

Chris.

PS   In regard to N.N. I was greatly disappointed in Albert not coming up to the scratch, and joining us.

PS   Your name is wrongly spelt in dedication of 'A Moment'—but I corrected that all right.—I hope you do not mind it appearing: or my use in 'Four Years' Harvest' of a little bit of one of your letters to me.[3]

---

1   *Annals of the Five Senses.*
2   The poems never appeared under this title, but may have been absorbed into volumes which were published at a later date.
3   'Four Years' Harvest' is one of the sketches in *Annals*. The lines from Ogilvie's letter appeared in the following passage:

> Not yet, if ever could he realise the desire a friend had expressed when he wrote, apropos of certain wildly unrelated manuscripts he had sent him from Salonika: 'There may be a method in your madness an old fogey like me cannot be expected to detect. I am ever in danger of under-rating the strength of tide in these new times, and of forgetting that your inconsequent excursions may subtly represent the many and diverse channels it is cutting out for itself in minds like yours. Still to continue the figure, I don't want your 'bore' to run to sea in a delta, but in a broad and navigable waterway wherein we may anchor one day to our great delight' (pp 66–7). The lines were first identified by J K Annand and confirmed by MacDiarmid. (See *Early Lyrics*, p 4.)

12 White's PLace, Montrose.

26 September 1921

Dear Mr Ogilvie,

Many thanks for you letter characteristically over-generous as usual. Despite the clearest realisation of my actual deserts I would have been disappointed had it been otherwise. Variety is the spice of life—and your letters are variety to me in that sense coming as they generally do between batches of editorial rejections and regrets. I put my best into my work. Neither in subject, treatment or any other way do I write to suit this paper or that or any purpose save my own reasonable satisfaction. So that I do not care whether you are a biased laudator or otherwise. If I please you that is almost enough for me—when I get more depressed than usual I even get defiantly proud of the fact that I am an author with a public of one, out-Landoring Landor[1] so—in any event such a letter as yours counterbalances right-away accumulating doubts and dejections of all kinds. Sometimes I re-read a whole batch of them until I purge myself of the presumption of disappointment and set to to write something spontaneously and unaccountably mine again utterly oblivious or contemptuous of the fact that it is 99 chances to 1 that it will be even more insusceptible of any editor's or publisher's acceptance. I enclose a poem just by way of example.[2] Squire of the *London Mercury*[3] wrote to me of it that he 'liked it—but didn't see that they could publish it'. Concerning another little poem[4] he said in the same letter that he would have taken it but they were so full up with accepted poems that a thing had to absolutely bowl them over before they could take it, in the meantime. He suggested that I should send this poem (this second one of which I am speaking) to the *Outlook*.[5] I have done so and await the result. – – – But obviously, his couldn't-ness in regard to this poem (which he did not advise me to try elsewhere—not even in the *British Weekly*!)[6] was based on considerations quite other than that overflowing drawer. He writes very exactly. 'Like' from him means a lot. Almost I can persuade myself that this poem did bowl him over, that he had a struggle with himself to refuse it, that his refusal is actually apologetic and shamefaced, and that he was actuated by sordid, horrible, and unmentionable reasons, philistine reasons, considerations of prudence and the fitness of things and les covenances.—But my poor little poem! In what way does it come under the operation of such considerations. I re-read it. If it is blasphemous then I do not know what blasphemy is, I—who upon occasion have tried to be deliberately blasphemous! If it is obscene, precisely where then? (It goes a long way beyond mere hermaphroditism of course).—You see my point, of course.—What I want to know is what Deity was likely to be enraged or outraged by its publication—Mammon, Mrs Grundy, or which of them?

Enough!—Seriously it is likely to mean a great deal to me in one way how these *Annals* go. If 2,000 copies sell all will be well. In other words I shall be able to get more work of the same sort published—and that's all I care about. I'm not limiting myself to its sort: but I have a lot of its sort I do want published: and I just want enough practical success to have as little difficulty as possible about that.—I have a feeling that if it doesn't go sufficiently well I shall be bound over to keep the peace and compelled to do so—gagged and bound—I have no wish to let the Cursed Commercial System turn me into

'some mute inglorious Milton'.[7]

—But it is necessary to remember that it may, and can, do so: and that if it decides to do so there is only one way in which the aspirant can avoid being reduced to impotence—and that's a way I refuse to take.

However, we'll see.

Yes! I am keeping rather splendid physically, or was, up to a week ago. In the interval I have almost boggled into jaundice again and am feeling still seismic and unsafe—but I think I'll be all right.

I am looking forward to seeing you soon. I think I may be in Edinr. about 7th October—but will let you know.

I was sorry to hear of Mrs Ogilvie's uncle's death: and of her own consequent unrobustness. I hope she may soon recover the vitality of which that trial robbed her.

With kindest regards from Mrs G and myself.

Yours Ever.

C. M. G.

NOTES

1 Walter Savage Landor (1775–1864). English writer and dramatist whose work has been claimed by an appreciative few to rank with the great achievements of literature, but is generally unread.
2 'The Universal Man'.
3 *See* letter 15 November 1920.
4 'Cattle Show'.
5 *The National Outlook.*
6 *The British Weekly*, a journal of 'Social and Christian Progress', published in London.
7 Thomas Gray's 'Elegy in a Country Churchyard' (1751):

Some mute inglorious Milton here may rest,
Some Cromwell guiltless of his country's blood.

The Universal Man
(To Lady Astor)[1]

Helen's white breasts are leaping yet,
The blood still drips from Jesus' feet,
All ecstasies and agonies
Within me meet.

Cyrenean and Pilate I,[2]
Centurion and Thief and Christ,
Still, in a thousand shapes, with Time
I keep my tryst.

Aphrodite, I rise again:
Eurydice, am drawn from Hell,
And lean across the bar of Heaven,
The Damozel

Yea and I sit in Parliament
For Plymouth and the Sphinx[3]
Who am what every newsboy shouts
And what God thinks!

and this is the one which on Squire's suggestion I sent to *The Outlook*.

Cattle Show

I shall go among red faces and virile voices,
See stylish sheep, with fine heads, and well-wooled,
And great bulls mellow to the touch,
Brood mares of marvellous approach, and geldings
With sharp and flinty bones and silken hair.

And through th' enclosure draped in red and gold
I shall pass to spheres more vivid yet
Where countesses' coque feathers gleam and glow,
And swathed in silks the painted women are[4]
Whose laughter plays like summer lightning there!

1 Nancy Witcher Langhorne Astor (Viscountess) (1879–1964). Born in Virginia, USA she succeeded her husband as MP for Plymouth in 1919 and was the first woman to take her place in the House of Commons.
2 In the published version lines one and two of this stanza are inverted.
3 In the published version this reads 'Portsmouth and the Sphinx' and is obviously an error, given that Nancy Astor's constituency was Plymouth.
4 In the published version this reads 'the painted ladies are'. There are minor changes in punctuation in the published versions of both poems.

                                              12 White's Place. Montrose.

14 October 1921

Dear Mr Ogilvie,

Your letter was a Godsend. It is weak of me but I do get atrociously depressed at times: and the worst of it is that I do so not without cause!

I shall be happy to advise Mr Watters[1] when the review copies are issued. It was very good of you to think of this.

It occurs to me now that if you care to do so and feel that you can—if you know Mr Watters sufficiently well—you might perhaps sound him as to the possibility of there being any opening or any likelihood of one in the near future on the *Scotsman* literary or Sub-Editorial staffs.

I have done very well here: But I have to work far too hard. I get practically no leisure. And the job is a cul-de-sac. It leads to nothing. My employer will testify to my unusual diligence, enterprise, competence, and reliability. He regards me as a perfect paragon and (without immodesty) rightly so—I *am* a rara avis in local journalism. Unfortunately any abilities I have are not called into play—this job only takes brute endurance, solid slogging, and routine experience.

Although I have meant for some time to seize the first Glasgow or Edinr. chance I could, I would not write to you but for another reason. Montrose is not agreeing with Mrs G I have to shift as soon as I can, somewhere. Now Edinr. does suit her—superlatively. So I can scarcely hesitate to explore the possibilities that lie in your acquaintanceship with Mr Watters. Such jobs are impossible to get without influence. I do not wish a reportorial job—but am willing to take anything on an editorial or literary staff. I have had a very extensive experience now and can prove thorough competence. Given a chance I shall certainly reward the giver by making thoroughly good. I need say no more. If Mr Watters could secure me an interview I could give all the necessary particulars etc.

Accept my best thanks for all you have done: and forgive my again trying to make use of you. It is wretched of me.

With kindest regards to Mrs Ogilvie, the children and yourself.

                                   Yours as ever.

                                   Chris.

PS   I had hoped to be in Edinr. on the 7th inst. but was unexpectedly prevented. But I shall see you soon I think. I intend if possible to take a week's holidays before the end of this month.

NOTES

1   George Watters, then editor of the *Scotsman*.

c/o Bryson,
109 High Street, Selkirk.

27 October 1921

Dear Mr Ogilvie,

Mrs G and I purpose spending a few hours in Edinburgh tomorrow—arriving from here 9.41 a.m. at Waverley.[1] I am hoping to see you.

I have spent a delightful week here and am feeling vastly the better of the change. The Border air suits me: and I am better among the hills than by the sea.

With kindest regards to Mrs Ogilvie and the children and to yourself.

Yours.

C M Grieve.

NOTES

1   The main railway station at Edinburgh.

12 White's Place, Montrose.

9 November 1921

Dear Mr Ogilvie,

I am tremendously indebted to you and to Mr Stewart for what you have done and tried to do for me.

I wish it had occurred to me that the old *Dispatch*[1] escapade—as you call it—had any such jack-in-the-box capacity: or that, even so, its sudden reappearance would have had the effect it has had. I would certainly not have rendered your efforts liable to any such frustration. I did not count upon its having been forgotten: on the contrary—so defective is my conscience—I had for all practical purposes forgotten about it myself and did not even recall it when thinking about the possibilities of a job on the *Scotsman*—far less take it into account as a potential factor.

Escapade by the way is absolutely the right term to apply.

From what you say – – – – 'after hearing his (Watters') account, we could not press him'—I gather that Mr Watters must have given you a more serious impression.

It may be that it would arm me against not impossible contingencies in the future (this incident clearly shows that anything is possible) to know exactly what he did say. You will know best whether you can tell me that or not however.

I do not underestimate the lack of humour in the world: but I cannot imagine Mr Watters to be as entirely devoid of it as to rule me out on account of that escapade if he knows the true facts. I have every reason to believe that he is 'punishing' me for a 'crime' I never committed—although I can quite well believe that he has what he thinks are the best of grounds for believing that I did.

It has been said that there is nothing more difficult than to forgive a person whom you have wronged. So I account for this attitude on the part of the *Scotsman*. For the Chief Reporter did a very cruel and, worse, a very stupid thing—and knew that I assessed his action at its correct value.

I write contemptuously, of course, – – – I do not suffer fools of a different type to my own gladly – – – but although I have no desire to 'vindicate my character' as the horrible phrase goes I cannot permit these people to convert me into 'a young man with a terrible past before me'—and I should appreciate an opportunity of pointing out that what they are doing amounts to criminal libel.

I could as a matter of fact have cleared up the matter at the time by bringing an action against the proprietors of the *Dispatch*—but, as you may remember I was very ill with jaundice at the time: and too contemptuous of the possible consequences to bother.

I thank you for expressing your continued trust in me and can only reassure you that I did nothing that I am in the least degree ashamed of and nothing that I cannot defend.

Did I say in my note that I would be in Edinr. on the Friday? If so I made a mistake in writing. It should have read Saturday at time stated. I was: and intended to have been in town all day—then caught last train here. Unfortunately Mrs G took ill: and I caught the next train for Methil[2] (her home) and stayed there over the week-end. Mrs G underwent a slight operation on Sunday—successfully: and is recovering nicely. I need not add that I was tremendously disappointed not to see you. I had been looking forward to a talk with you for weeks.

I will see what Buchan can do. What Watters says about scope for men like me in the provinces no one knows better than I do. I have no delusions. Only I hoped that I might get something where the drudgery might be less unadulterated than here, the leisure slightly longer, in some centre where I would have a better library at my disposal than here, and, preferably in Edinburgh because Edinr. suits Mrs G and—for my own part—because you are there.

However please do not worry! I shall be all right in the long run. Such an attitude towards an ancient and entirely trivial 'irregularity' as you discovered in Mr Watters confirms me in all my best suspicions. It has quite bucked me up. Nothing is better calculated to renew in me the determination to make good in my own way than such dreadful examples of moral obscenity.

You will appreciate that I am not writing flippantly,—but, on the contrary, passionately. 'For the moment' you say 'we looked foolish'. I can quite imagine your real feelings: and writhe in impotence at the thought. But – – – my time will come. And I think I will be able some day to write such an account of the *Dispatch* episode and this belated phase of it as will make 'the other side' look infinitely more foolish. I will judge my my judge (d.v.)[3] with a vengeance.

I cannot understand why *N.N.* and *Annals* are not out. I wired Foulis yesterday to find out but have received no reply yet. The delay is inexplicable and most unfortunate.

Again with all thanks to Mr Stewart and yourself: and kindest regards to Mrs Ogilvie and yourself.

Yours Ever.

C. M. G.

NOTES

1 The *Edinburgh Evening Dispatch* where MacDiarmid had worked as a reporter in 1911.
2 A seaport in Fife, located near Wemyss on the north shore of the Firth of Forth.
3 *Deo volente*—God willing.

This letter is misdated. As the content follows on directly from the preceding letter, the probable date is 25 November 1921.

Montrose.

25 September 1921 [25 November 1921?]

Dear Mr Ogilvie,

I am sorry that it has been impossible for me to reply earlier, owing to troubles of various sorts which have more than monopolized my time and energy.

My last letter was of course never intended to be taken literally. I merely meant to give you such a reply as you might show to Mr Watters. I quite understood that the whole business was inviolably private and, in 'asking' for it, know perfectly well that you could not and would not give any more than I could use any statement as to what Mr Watters actually did tell you.

My point is this—that the *Dispatch* made no charge against me at all: nor did I admit any offence. No reason was assigned for my dismissal—nor was any asked. I was too ill at the time both in body and in mind to show fright to circumstance or protect myself in any way from consequence.

I concluded from your letter (not the last one) that Mr Watters gave you the impression that, to say the least of it, my dismissal was justifiable. I suggest that after all these years it is surprising that he should remember with such particularity what was, however, regarded, at worst a very minor misdemeanour: and question if he remembers correctly. I could not, I am afraid, disguise from the very first that I considered Donald, the chief reporter of the *Dispatch*, a very obnoxious kind of fool. I afflicted him in ways you can no doubt imagine with an intolerable sense of his inferiority, mentally at any rate—and he avenged himself when opportunity arose. I do not blame him for that. But I ought to have seen that he did not magnify the matter. I ought to have seen that he was rendered incapable of transmitting more than the exact facts – – – which probably he did not know himself.

What actually did happen was this. I did some book reviewing on the *Dispatch*. My wage left practically nothing over after paying my 'digs'. I was anxious to get on. I was trying to do free-lance articles in my spare time. I found it very difficult indeed to buy the necessary paper, envelopes and stamps to send them on their rounds. I got practically no return except in rejection slips. It was borne in upon me that the cause of this was that my articles were not typed. The cost of having them typed was a problem. I thought however that if I could surmount this difficulty it was only a question of time before I would 'arrive'. As books for review were handed to me I reviewed them—then sold them to second-hand shops— getting a few shillings for each which I used to get my stuff typed and sent out. I ordered the same books at a booksellers and when they came gave them to the *Dispatch*. The effect was that I was getting the ready money I needed to carry on my literary efforts—while my account for books was mounting up. But I did not go too far. I knew that the acceptance of one or two articles would bring in sufficient to wipe out that account—perhaps to leave me even with a balance which would enable me to discontinue the unprofitable practise circumstances had compelled me to adopt—and I did not let my account mount beyond what could be so covered. I did get one or two articles accepted: but only for small sums: and one or two books I was accordingly able to pay cash for.

If I had had a little luck all would have been well—so I told myself, gambler-wise. I would have cleared my account at the booksellers, the *Dispatch* would not have suffered in the least—and would have had ordinary copies indeed of the books in question instead of copies stamped 'for review'—a slight gain!

But I was doing, or trying, too much and collapsed: I had a serious illness—jaundice.

The position then was that I owed a pound or two to the booksellers—and that all the review copies I had had from the *Dispatch* had been replaced except one. The copy to replace that one had not been delivered when I took ill.

What transpired during my illness I do not know. But what I had been doing was discovered—somehow. At least I suppose so. Precisely what construction was put upon it I do not know—the worst, judging by the result—and Donald was incapable of anything else in any case. I returned to the office as soon as I was convalescent—ridiculously glad to get back to work—and was dismissed.

In the outcome the *Dispatch* did not lose a single copy and I paid the bookseller in full.

Was there theft or any other crime in what I did? I plead guilty only to unsuccess. Perhaps I should have 'bided a wee'[1]—waited till my wages increased—or saved a penny or two a week to enable me to submit an article a year to one or perhaps two editors?

I hope that I have put matters clearly. It is the truth, *the whole truth*, and nothing but the truth. I did not, for instance, get the books from the bookseller on false pretences—pretending that I was ordering them on behalf of the *Dispatch* or anything like that.

The essence of my position was the belief that if I could only get one or two of my articles taken I could even up the difference between what I received from the review copies from the second-hand bookseller, and what I paid for the others to replace them.

Selling the review copies gave me working capital: getting the others on account gave me the necessary time.

I will only add that I am still convinced so absurdly sanguine is the temperament with which I am accursed that I could have at any time between then and now have made good as a free-lance writer if I had even been in such a position that I had sufficient leisure and an appropriate environment to work in and sufficient spare cash to get my stuff typed and kept going the rounds.

But my mental and physical energy has also been so fully absorbed by drudgery—and my instincts so browbeaten and cowed by philistine surroundings—that I have had little time or heart to devote to original writing (apart from the other inherent difficulties): and I have never been able to afford to maintain a regular bombardment upon editorial entrenchments.

Apart from all else I knew then—and I know now—that I was *legally entitled to retain the Review books in question and to dispose of them as I thought fit*. I reviewed them and the law would be on my side if I claimed that ipso facto they were mine. So it is criminal libel if I am charged with having dishonestly sold review copies belonging to the *Dispatch*.

I do not accept your formula—simply because a formal application would only evoke a formal answer regretting that there was no vacancy—and we would be no forrader.[2]

But I shall not do—or write—anything that can ever put any friend into any such position as my letter led Mr Stewart to imagine he or Mr Watters might occupy.

Disappointments continue without intermission. I have just been informed that the publication of *Annals* has been indefinitely postponed.

Excuse this scrawl and my delay. Believe me deeply appreciative of your unfailing sympathy and understanding.

Yours Ever.

C M Grieve.

PS   Let me add, too, that I perfectly realise that the only victory is for me to make good as you put it, in the Big Way – – – and let me reassure you in the most absolute sense of the words that no matter what trials and troubles of external or internal circumstance still await me, I shall—abundantly—dispite the fact that art is always getting longer and life shorter.[3]

NOTES

1   'bided my time'.
2   'No further ahead'.
3   *Ars longa, vita brevis.* (Seneca: *De Brevitate Vitae*)

12 White's Place. Montrose.

29 December 1921

Dear Mr Ogilvie,

Please excuse again my writing in pencil, and my delay in replying to your last two kind letters—a delay due to the fact that I have been more than usually 'busy', an excuse which is none the less sincere despite the fact that I have been busy for the most part only in a cerebral sense. My most urgent affairs (to which haplessly I sacrifice all other considerations) continue to be almost entirely psychological. I am really very robust. I was deeply concerned to hear that you yourself were off colour: I hope you have recovered. You will now be on holiday, glad, I know, of the respite, which I hope will be thoroughly profitable in health, as in other, respects.

N.N. 2 is going splendidly. The reviews I have so far seen are very favourable but of course hopelessly meritical—enough to make one follow Robert Buchanan's[1] example and in sheer desperation review oneself. They are on the whole longer than last year's and more wholly commendatory. I will certainly send you my collection.

Despite the weekly *Scotsman's* opinion that 'some of Mr Grieve's sonnets are as difficult of access as the mountains which inspired them'[2] and the *Edinr. Evening News'* remark that 'they breathe the real tang of the heather',[3] my own work has attracted this year far more attention from people whose opinion counts a little with me. Mrs Violet Jacob[4] singles out my *'admirable* Edinburgh' and Agnes Falconer[5] says 'Nothing in the volume is more attractive to me than your own extraordinary little poem 'Edinburgh'—an etching in a few lines in which the spiritual and the picturesque are powerfully blended. No one who reads this will easily forget it'. Miss Symon[6] says 'Your things are powerful—very' and intimates that on the strength of their appeal she has ordered a copy of *Annals*— which a literary friend of her own had told her was 'a remarkable work'. I wonder who the prophet was. *Annals* will be out early in the Spring. Delay was due to Mr Foulis's sudden collapse. He is now back to business. Probably it's all for the best. Review space will be more generously obtainable then.

I have been conducting a further stage of my guerrilla warfare with the Vernacular Circle of the London Burns Club in the columns of the *Aberdeen Free Press*.[7] J M Bulloch, editor of the *Graphic* is my opposite number. The dispute arose out of a paper he gave on 'The Delight of the diminutive in the Doric'. I replied with a few scornful phrases about 'Doric Infantilism'. He responded with a full column of Fleet Street paternalism—as one who still grieved over the Henley-Stevenson business.[8] I have replied again—to the effect that I believe that 'progress in sexual ethics is at length removing the "specific aboulia" so long responsible for the prevalence of the diminutive in Scotland' and that Burns like Christ[9] (with whom he shares the distinction of having his birthday celebrated all over the world) is a mere eponym giving his name to a cult entirely at variance with his own spirit—as a result of being subjected to a system of syncretism—the consequence being that Burnsism now is 'an unique abnormality of mob psychology, pickled in whisky', interesting only to students of literary pathology.

All this of course has its effect on *N.N.* If *N.N.* isn't a movement it will be. A group is going to emerge. The relations between Ferguson, and others, and myself are greatly strengthened, let drop out who will—or must. There will be enough left to go ahead. Short of unintelligibility I am more than ever determined to act on the 'Left Wing'. I shall shortly send you the draft of a long poem entitled 'Water of Life',[10] the first two sections of which I have now complete—this is a preliminary credo: and I am also working hard at a sequence of poems on Edinburgh which I intend to make a complete and quite portly book of, entitled 'Sic Itur ad Astra'[11] (the city motto)—I have been moved to

this by a perusal of Rosaline [*sic*] Masson's anthology *In Praise of Edinburgh*[12]—
Edinburgh has never been praised either in prose or poetry—the poems given are
horrible in the extreme. I do not flatter myself at all when I say that my own
wee 'Edinburgh' is ten times better than anything in that burdensome tome.

Had a most encouraging and kind letter from Stewart.

Mrs Grieve joins me in wishing Mrs Ogilvie and the children and yourself all
happiness in the coming years.

With love.

Chris.

NOTES

1 Robert Williams Buchanan (1841–1901), born at Averswall, Staffordshire, but
   educated in Glasgow. Famous for his 'The Fleshly School of Poetry' (1871), which
   was an attack on the poetry of the Pre-Raphaelites. He wrote criticism under a
   number of pseudonyms and reviewed his own work, practices which MacDiarmid
   did adopt.
2 Reviewed in the *Scotsman*, 19 December 1921, p 3.
3 Reviewed in the *Edinburgh Evening News* 13 December 1921, p 7.
4 Violet Jacob (1863–1946), Scottish poet and novelist, best known for her poems in
   dialect and short stories. She was later recognised by MacDiarmid as one of the
   'heralds' of the vernacular revival and her contributions to *N.N.* 1 and 2 were highly
   praised by him. Poems: *Verses* (1905), *Songs of Angus* (1915), *More Songs of Angus*
   (1918). See MacDiarmid's article on her work in *C.S.S.*, pp 8–10.
5 Agnes Falconer, Scottish poet who was also included in *N.N.* 2. Poems: *Wishing
   Wood and other Verses* (1911).
6 Mary Symon (1863–1938), Scottish poet whose poems in the vernacular were
   included in *N.N.* 2. Poems: *Deveron Days* (1933). One of the features of *N.N.* 2 was
   the high representation of women poets.
7 On 13 December 1921, the *Aberdeen Free Press* published an article on the paper
   which James Malcolm Bulloch (1867–1938), (editor of *The Graphic* from 1909–1924)
   had given to the Vernacular Circle of the London Burns Club, the title of which was
   'Diminutives in the Doric'. A letter from MacDiarmid was published on 15
   December (quotations from which follow) which attacked Bulloch's claim that the
   'diminutive' expressed the 'national mentality', dismissing it as 'Doric infantilism'.
   Bulloch replied on 21 December, stating that as one who had witnessed 'Henley
   bludgeon Stevenson' he did not want to enter into any debate which would end in a
   literary schism. On 23 December, MacDiarmid replied, stating that there was a new
   spirit abroad in Scottish poetry which would shake off the limitations of the
   'diminutive' and free itself from the slavish imitation of Burns. The debate was very
   lively and attracted attention with MacDiarmid subsequently pursuing in other
   papers and journals his attack on the Burns cult.
8 W E Henley and Robert Louis Stevenson were friends and literary collaborators, but
   their friendship ended bitterly over Henley's questioning of the authorship of a short
   story by Stevenson's wife. Henley subsequently attacked Stevenson's work, but later

tried to renew the friendship. Stevenson, however, rejected his approaches and they remained at odds with each other.

9   The comparison between Burns and Christ is pursued in *A Drunk Man.*
10 Published in *N.N.* 3 (see *C.P.* II, pp 1213-5). This was MacDiarmid's earliest attempt at a long poem and it is notable for its erotic imagery.
11 Such is the way to the stars (Virgil, *Aeniad*, ix, 641).
12 Rosaleen Masson (d. 1949). Scottish author who wrote mainly histories. *In Praise of Edinburgh: An Anthology in Prose and Verse* (Constable) 1912.

Note new address:-
16 Links Avenue. Montrose.

19 March 1922

Dear Mr Ogilvie,

I have been intending to write you for weeks now—so strange and insupportable your long silence! I have wondered and worried. Of course I know how incessantly too-busy you are: but, then, anything else might have happened also—illness—anything. Do drop me a note soon. All my own correspondence is in arrears—for a variety of reasons. Mr Stewart, in particular, deserved a letter long before this. I shall write him soon. Today I am just emerging from the turmoil of a flitting. Hitherto we have perforce been in a furnished house. A new house was allocated to us months ago: but took much longer to build than could be anticipated—as is always the case. However it is ready now: and we got our furniture in the day before yesterday and yesterday I had to be as energetic a spectator as I could possibly contrive while Mrs G did the work of getting the place into order. So thoroughly did I fill my rôle, in fact, that I was very much more tired at the end of the day than she was: and today I am one of those pictures that tell stories—only my story is (although no one would think so to look at me) one of those kind which can only be properly articulated with one's tongue in one's cheek and the pupil of one eye at an angle of 30 degrees to the line of vision of the other.

The fact is that I have nothing but domesticities to relate. Since I wrote you last (but this too is deplorably domestic as well) I have become a member of Montrose Town Council[1] and have thrown myself with more energy than I imagined I possessed into the work of Local Government. I have also blossomed out as one of the leaders of the Scottish Free State Movement[2] and have addressed a public meeting in Dundee, issued a public challenge to an Arbroath opponent, conducted an incredible variety of newspaper controversies, etc. etc.[3]

Apart from that however I have been busy. I cannot tell you all about my different projects here. But I want to tell you about one. I have planned a book of 100 sonnets.[4] I have over 40 of them written:- i.e. written in their final form, which I cannot improve. Others are in draft or I am more dissatisfied with them as yet than with the 40. All of them are obscure in at least one, and generally in more than one, respect. They deal with foreign subjects—Russian, French, Italian, Spanish, Bulgarian—for the most part:[5] and are largely unintelligible to those who are not thoroughly familiar with the modern literatures of these countries. They are highly allusive—but I am supplying notes which will be interesting in themselves and thoroughly illuminating. I cannot apologise for obscurity of this kind. Some of them derive additional 'obscurity' from the fact that they seek to express in concentrated form as it were the essence of the paradoxical philosophies of Blake, Nietzsche,[6] etc. Again there are cases in which the fundamental metaphor cannot be understood without a knowledge of certain foreign ceremonies—i.e. in one sonnet the ceremony of Cursing and Expulsion from a Jewish synagogue is used as a basis. No one can understand this sonnet who doesn't know what a Sharof is etc.[7]—but to Jews it will be perfectly clear.

I have nowhere sought obscurity for obscurity's sake. To certain classes of readers—i.e. students of the literatures in question—these sonnets will all be perfectly clear. They all fit into one big scheme. What moved me in the first place to write them was Croce's[8] statement as to the necessity of reckoning systemmatically [sic] with the enormous accumulation of moral doubts and psychological perceptions in the 19th Century—and the impossibility of thinking we can transcend them by merely being contemptuous and dismissing them as Mid-Victorian. That—and Clutton Brock's[9] statement that art must be a desperate adventure—if not it ceases to be art and becomes merely a game of skill.

I think I have written my best sonnets so far in this sequence. I enclose a few upon which I beg you to give me your candid opinion.[10] I have chosen the less recondite because I have not time yet to write out the explanatory notes which must accompany the others. But what do you think of these? I again emphasize that they were largely written for you—apart from other considerations the necessity of ultimately justifying your faith in me determines my efforts.

Excuse more in the meantime. Do please write soon and tell me how you are. *Annals* should be out very soon now. It has been a terrible wait. However all's well that ends well.

Mrs G joins me in conveying every good wish.

Ever Yours.

Chris.

NOTES

1 MacDiarmid was elected to Montrose Town Council as an Independent Socialist.
2 There was no movement of that name in Scotland, but MacDiarmid is probably referring to the Scottish Home Rule Association which he had joined in 1920. The SHRA had been a pre-war movement which had been reconstituted in 1918 by Roland Eugene Muirhead who had been on the old council, and Tom Johnston, MP, a member of the ILP and editor of *Forward*.
3 MacDiarmid had earlier contributed articles to the SHRA newsheet, but he began to intensify his activities during this period, publishing controversial articles in a number of periodicals and newspapers.
4 MacDiarmid published some of these sonnets (with footnotes) in *S.C.*: 'J. K. Huysmans', 'In the Golden Island', 'Amiel', 'Of Two Bulgarian Poets', *'Introduzione alla Vita Mediocre'* appeared in November 1922 issue and *'U Samago Moria'*, *'Der Wunderrabiner von Barcelona'* and *'Miguel de Unamuno'* in March 1923 issue.
5 Part of MacDiarmid's interest in European literature was to present it as an alternative influence to the English tradition. He often introduced lines in various languages into his poems, and often exaggerated his knowledge of languages.
6 The idea of the clash of opposites—Blake's 'contraries without which there is no progression' and Nietzsche's Apollo—Dionysos antithesis—is of a piece with MacDiarmid's own dialectical aesthetic, the Caledonian Antisyzygy.
7 No poem dealing with this subject was ever published. The only specifically Jewish theme in this sequence is *'Der Wunderrabiner von Barcelona'*, but it contains no reference to the ceremony of expulsion.
8 Benedetto Croce (1866–1952), Italian philosopher, historian, critic and politician whose aesthetic theories were published in his major philosophical work, *Lo Spirito*. Croce defended nineteenth-century liberalism and humanistic education and argued that art needs religious and ethical ideas. *See* MacDiarmid's article, 'Croce and Certain European Writers' in *The New Age*, 2 October 1924, pp 271–2.
9 Arthur Clutton-Brock (1868–1924), English journalist, critic and essayist. He was considerably influenced by Croce's ideas and popularised them in various articles he wrote for *The Speaker* and *The Times*, which were later collected in *Essays on Art* (1918) and *Essays on Books* (1920). The idea of art as 'a desperate adventure' expresses the theme of an article in which MacDiarmid set out his early aesthetic 'Art and the Unknown', *The New Age*, 20 and 27 May 1926) where the artist is represented as a pioneer of new territories of experience and works for the 'extension of consciousness'.
10 No poems have been retained with this letter.

The letter which follows is undated but given the reference to the sonnets seems to follow on from the preceding one.

16 Links Avenue

[March 1922?]

Dear Mr Ogilvie,

No! I don't like your figure of the anchor. Rather let us say that you are an old friend—the oldest and best of friends—who has travelled far in and become familiar with the seas of thought in which I, who have hitherto been a coaster, am sometime to navigate this new type of ship of mine (let me admit since you insist upon it that you know less than I do about this kind of ship—or the ultimate purpose of my voyage—although in the latter respect I must in turn insist that I am under sealed orders!)—Your query as to whether I was not overrating Amiel's importance, your criticism of the implied proposal to systemmatize poetry, etc., all these are so many hints as to cross-currents, 'snags' and the like. It is these things I so wish I could discuss with you—or with anyone in any way like you: I am exiled from my element here in this respect. - - 'The artist has no right to complain if he is misunderstood by the large mass of his contemporaries. But he has the right to expect to be comprehended by a few. - - Poe's[2] isolation in America was of this unhappy and stultifying kind and its effect upon his poetry are plain. For the most remarkable thing about him as a poet is the contrast between his scanty production—and the natural facility, the unmistakeable fecundity, of his poetic genius. - - - Keats without his £2000, Shelley without his private income, would they, we wonder, have written more, or more finely, than Poe? But they would at least have been sustained by a handful of understanding friends. It does not appear that Poe had one'.

Without flattering comparisons of my own case with Poe's—I have at least one: and I object to him calling himself an anchor - - - an anchor anxious to see the ship dispense with its services and be off!

Your letters mean a great deal to me—and, apart from all that, you are one of my very oldest friends and I was genuinely anxious to hear how you were keeping—apart from the delight of your letters always give me—a delight I disassociate from the sensations produced by the fact that they refer to me and my work and your hopes and fears for me and my work, and find [it] has a splendid independent existence, derived from the fact that these are the letters of a friend, and the letters of one of the very few friends one encounters nowadays who can write letters.

No more in the meantime. My sonnets continue to accumulate. My real reason for sonneteering instead of writing in other forms is that I want to write two or three sonnets which will live—which will rank with the great sonnets of British literature—and once I do write two or three sonnets which a competent critic assures me fill that bill I shall stop sonneteering. The sonnet form is not natural to me. But I won't be beaten by the 'demned little thing'.—Once I win I will proceed with all expedition to tackle other forms.

But I am not by any means confining myself to the sonnet as matters stand.

And this note is merely to thank you for your letter and to enclose this longer poem[3] upon which I want just two or three words of opinion.

Mrs G joins me in kindest regards to Mrs Ogilvie, the children, and yourself.

Yours Ever.

C. M. G.

PS   Will you please return the MS? I've no copy—and am too lazy to write one out.

NOTES

1 *See* 'Amiel' (*C.P.* II, pp 1218–9), also letter 20 August 1916.
2 Edgar Allan Poe (1809–1849). The quotation marks suggest that these lines are from a secondary source which is, however, unidentified.
3 'From *Water of Life*'.

16 Links Avenue, Montrose.

5 April 1922

Dear Mr Ogilvie,

The discovery that two recent letters of mine to different friends have not been received by them makes me anxious to know if you duly received my last letter containing MSS of a longish poem 'Water of Life'—of which foolishly enough, I took no copy (owing to laziness).

I particularly hope this MSS is safe in your hands. The poem is like the parson's egg—good only in parts—but I am anxious not to lose it.

I know you must be very busy just now—Quarterlies, etc., I suppose—and perhaps that accounts for your not writing yet, even if you have safely received it.

I am not trying to hustle any reply out of you—but I cannot shake off the feeling that in this particular case you have not received my letter and its enclosure.

Please drop me a p.c. just to say whether the poem reached you or not.

This worry serves me right. I mustn't be so lazy in the future and must take copies of my poems before entrusting them to the Postal Authorities.

Kindest regards

Yours Ever.

C M Grieve.

PS   I posted the letter in question a week past Friday.

16 Links Avenue. Montrose.

22 May 1922

Dear Mr Ogilvie,

Many thanks for you last letter. I am making various alterations on 'Water of Life'. I think they will immensely improve it.

Foulis has now succeeded in transforming his firm into a Limited Coy: and in a note yesterday promises me a definite decision within a week as to whether they can or can't undertake *N.N.* 3 this autumn. If they can't then I'll either get another publisher or bring it out myself.[1] In any case I am determined to go on with it.

I enclose copy of a circular which I am sending out to such and such as such.[2] My letters on the matter to the dailies last Monday evoked a splendid response. As you will see the G. *Herald* went the length of giving us a fine fillip in a leader.[3] So we're getting on.

But the difficulties of running such a periodical as I intend are immense: and if it is not to appear in miserably attenuated shape, but in substantial and worthy form, literally *every* Scottish poetry-lover must be roped in.

Since I wrote you last I have written over 40,000 words of a new novel— somewhat Henry Jamesy perhaps—but quite publishable I think.[4] I intend finishing it in time to permit of its being considered for autumn publication.

Oh! and that reminds me, Foulis promises final arrangements about *Annals* within the course of this week!!

Excuse this scrappy note: but I am of course nearly snowed under with correspondence in connection with this *Chapbook* business. But I wanted to drop you a note because I am sure that if there is anybody within reach you can persuade to subsidise creative literature in Scotland to the extent of some 2 ½d. per week in this way you'll want to have the chance of doing it. And I want to enrol as many subscribers as possible as soon as I possible [*sic*]—for I want to curtail the circulation immediately I see my way to cover costs. The arrangements I am making ensure that immediate bibliographical value will attend the first years issues anyhow. But I am not to disclose these details—subscribers will find that, apart from literary value, they have made a good investment.—Enough! I am in great form. With kindest regards to Mrs Ogilvie, the children, and yourself, in which Mrs G joins me.

Yours Ever.

C. M. G.

NOTES

1 MacDiarmid did publish it from Montrose in December 1922.
2 There is no circular attached to the letter, but it obviously refers to his latest publishing venture *The Scottish Chapbook*.
3 The leader appeared on 16 May 1922 and urged support for *The Scottish Chapbook* as a showcase for 'modern Scottish verse'. A letter by MacDiarmid had appeared in the *Glasgow Herald* on 15 May 1922, p 7, which had described the project as a platform for 'experimental poetics'.
4 MacDiarmid refers again to this work in the letter of 15 January 1923, but no novel of this period has yet come to light.

16 Links Avenue. Montrose.

[Post-card]
16 June 1922

Dear Mr Ogilvie,

I hope you duly received the two proofs of my photo: and found one or other suitable for the very flattering purpose intended.[1] I know you must be busy (I hope not ill, at any rate) but if you could drop me a note as to the subscribers you have succeeding [*sic*] in obtaining for the *Chapbook* I should be glad, as I have now secured more than the minimum number required and am anxious, in proceeding to make all the other multifarious arrangements for launching the venture in August, to know just how many are to comprise my list.—Will write at length in a day or two! Many thanks and every good wish.

Yours.

Grieve.

[Address on verso: Geo Ogilvie, Esq, MA, 14 St Catherine's Place, Edinburgh.]

NOTE

1 For inclusion in the Summer edition of *Broughton Magazine* which was running articles on former editors.

[Letterhead: *The Scottish Chapbook*]

16 Links Avenue.

20 September 1922

Dear Mr Ogilvie,

I should have written you a long ere this: but have been, and remain, overwhelmed. Going off to Birmingham in the beginning of the month to tell the Burns Federation a few things did not help matters. I had a glorious and most useful time: but have not yet made up the arrears of correspondence which accumulated in my absence. I have various other lecture-dates cutting into my time shortly—then, in February, am speaking to the Vernacular Circle in London. I have determined to transform the Burns movement at home and abroad: and am conducting an extensive and very subtle press campaign to that end. My slogan is—'the application of the spirit of Burns to practical affairs', 'first things first—would Burns have wasted time on bibliography, textual researches, genealogical investigations with Scotland in its present terrible social condition'; 'the realisation of the full social and political programme implicit in Burns' works', etc. etc.—I have constructed so many phrases that I am like a merry-go-round myself—but I am open to wager that over 30 columns of 'Burns Movement Re-Orientation' stuff appears in the press within the next six months.[1] I was the 'stormy petrel' at the Brum Conference but the September *Chapbook* will give you an indication of what I am driving at in this connection.[2]

I am also busy with the Scottish Home Rule business—and expect to be very much busier this winter yet. The October Assocn. newsheet will eulogise 'my work for Scottish literature' next month:[3] and in November will 'splash' a special article of mine on 'Scottish Home Rule and a Revival of Letters'.[4]

The *Chapbook* has gone splendidly. Sold out. Unable to supply scores of copies ordered. Roped in all sorts of desirable Scots from Stornoway to Hong Kong, Sunderland to New York.

Many thanks for your valuable letter on No. 1. Glad you were interested in *Nisbet*.[5] Haven't got a full sheaf of reviews but enclose a batch herewith. A mixed lot. But I know now exactly how much to attach to each—who writes them, etc.

I was greatly delighted with *Broughton Mag*. Many thanks. I came out quite well. Splendid photo of Kerr. Had letter from Editor[6] (still unanswered, alas! but will answer soon) asking for article for next number. Barkis is willin!7 Will try to let him have it soon. Something quite short. Will you please tell him so?

Yes. Just heard from Mr Stewart, with 10/- [10s. 0d.]. Many thanks for cheque for £2.10 [£2.10s.]. What about postage? Would it not be better for me to send to the 5 direct rather than trouble you?

Please excuse this scrappiest of letters. Hope you, Mrs Ogilvie and the children had a good holiday and are fine and fit. I am in notorious form myself. Do wish I could see you and have a talk: but may do so at no distant date. Many many thanks!

Yours Ever.

Chris.

NOTES

1 MacDiarmid contributed articles to the *Glasgow Herald*, the *Scottish Home Rule Newsheet*, the *Scots Pictorial* and many other journals and newspapers in this period. He wrote for the *Dunfermline Press* an extended series of articles entitled 'A Scotsman Looks at his World' which began in November 1922, and for the *Aberdeen Free Press* a series, 'A Scottish Theory of Literature', which began in August 1922.
2 The Burns Federation Conference was held at Birmingham on 1 and 2 September 1922 and MacDiarmid reported on it in 'At Birmingham', *S.C.*, September 1922, pp 38–44.
3 The October 1922 issue of the *Scottish Home Rule Newsheet* reviewed *S.C.*, describing it as 'a Scottish counterpart of Mr Squire's *London Mercury*'.
4 The article 'Scottish Literature and Home Rule' appeared in the newsheet for November 1922, pp 25–6.
5 Appeared in August and September editions of *S.C.*
6 The editor was then Albert David Mackie (1904–1985). Writer, journalist and poet, he later became editor of the *Edinburgh Evening News*.
7 From Charles Dickens's *David Copperfield*.

[Letterhead: *The Scottish Chapbook*]

10 October 1922

Dear Mr Ogilvie,

Excuse just the hastiest line in reply to your welcome note of 8th inst. to hand today.

I must have expressed myself most clumsily: for you have taken up my last letter in a different sense altogether to what I intended. 10/- [10s. 0d] is *Chapbook* cost per annum to original subscribers *post free*. It would be slightly more expensive to send out your five copies individually: I merely suggested it to save you trouble—I know you are busy enough. Then I didn't know whether the five were living near or whether you might have to repost the copies on to them, thus involving you in expense. What I meant about the postage was what if anything I owed you in respect of postage. You owed me nothing. I accordingly return stamps herewith.

I quite agree with you as to format of *Chapbook*. There are difficulties about changing it: but I shall do so at the earliest possible opportunity.

I enclose cutting of article from *Glasgow Herald*[1] you may not have seen. Also others. Please return when you write again.

Excuse this horrible scrawl. I am up to the first wrinkle on my many-seamed brow—above the eyebrows—in work of all sorts.

Kindest regards.

Yours. As Ever,

Chris.

NOTE

1 Possibly a cutting of the article by MacDiarmid, 'An Appeal to Scottish Poetry Lovers', which appeared in *Glasgow Herald* 15 May 1922.

16 Links Avenue, Montrose

15 January 1923

Dear Mr Ogilvie,

Quite unexpectedly—bereavement calling Mrs G in another direction—I did not manage to get further south than Kirkcaldy[1] at Christmas and New Year. I was quite disappointed to lose the chance of seeing you. But I shall certainly see you next month—either as I go to or return from London. And will have a good talk over things.

Your casual mention of Kerr's P.P.[2]—all you said was that you supposed I had heard of it—was the first I learned of it. But the weekend before last a mutual friend, Soutar,[3] who writes for the *Chapbook* and *N.N.* spent a few days with me and told me precisely what it was. Then I was speaking in Dundee last Thursday (Scottish Free State) and met Lewis Spence[4] who also spoke of it. I haven't seen the first issue, or any prospectus, or newspaper reference. I am writing Kerr by this post, however, enclosing what I understand to be the subscription for twelve issues—in the hope that I am still in time. I am sorry to learn from you that they are in a struggling state, finding their enterprise a burden, and doubtful if they will win through. I have, as you may imagine, absolutely no wish to 'butt in' where I am not wanted—but if it is merely lack of sufficient subscribers I think I could put them all right. Of course it may not be that—5/- [5s. 0d.] may be too little—and an increase of subscribers might worsen instead of better their position. Under the circumstances I cannot see my way to make direct inquiries as to the nature of their difficulties. But I am of course eager to help if I may. Can you send me a paragraph about it for insertion in the *Chapbook*?—by return if possible, as I am issuing the *Chapbook* a little earlier this month. I do not expect that that will help materially, however, though it will certainly make a few ask to become subscribers. If my own subscription is accepted and I get the first broadsheet, I will devote an article or two to the subject in certain papers and I can get helpful paragraphs inserted in certain quarters where they are likely to be influential. But direct appeal is the thing and I am in touch with plenty of people certain to subscribe. If this would help, can you procure copies of any prospectus or announcement-sheet or anything? If so, I would send them out.—But, if you do this, please tell whoever you get them from merely that you want them for a friend who has a notion that he can rope in a good few subscribers. Don't mention my name to Kerr or anybody else as willing to help, or in any way interested in, the *Chapbook*.

The weekly is coming all right.[5] I am absolutely up to the neck in preliminary arrangements. The whole story is too involved—but I *do* see my way financially and otherwise. I am in touch with nearly all the right people: and pulling all sorts of Labour Party,[6] Scottish Home Rule Assocn., Scots National League,[7] etc. strings. I am not yet quite sure when I will launch it—probably the beginning of March: but that will depend upon the final arrangements I make in London.

Annals has encountered another hitch. But don't worry. Either the people who have it in type just now must print it and let me publish it within the next week or two—or I'll have it set up here de novo and publish it. My lawyers have the matter well in hand now. But it has been a ghastly business.

A lot of people have written to me more or less as you do—as to the desirability of expounding my theories clearly and straightforwardly in the Causerie.[8] And I am to devote the next six causeries to that.

I was glad you were interested in *Nisbet*. I will have my draft typed as soon as I can—in full—and let you have a read of it. Also progress is being made now with the typing of my novel:[9] and if you are hard up for something to read during next Summer holidays, let me know!

I have just read over what you wrote about Kerr's P.P. and what I have just written. I hope I need not say that I bear Kerr no grudge of any kind at all and that I wish anything he may try unbounded success. Only—while extremely eager to help him if I possibly can—I would prefer that he should not know that I was doing so. I do not wish to be associated by name in any case with his work—although I do not know what you mean at all when you say 'his ways are not exactly yours, and v.v.'

Press reviews of *N.N.* 3 have been very good—heaps of very encouraging letters from people from whom encouragement is worth having—sales by no means satisfactory to date—but I'm not worrying.

Now I must knock off. I'm 'bunged up' with cold and nasal catarrh, and so my daily output is not quite what it should be. And I have vowed to at least treble it this year—in every direction. I intend to sling out MSS of all sorts in 'every airt the wind can blaw'[10]—by all sorts I mean political, and literary articles, short stories etc.—work worth doing all the time, however, and not mere pot-boilers. I have not been pestering editors as I should have done: but I have been accumulating and I am ready at last to disgorge.

Excuse this scrappy note. I hope you have fully recovered and that this may find Mrs Ogilvie and the children in good condition. Please remember me to any friends.

Yours faithfully,

C M Grieve.

PS   Mackie (A.D.) is coming on! He has sent some sonnets and some dialect stuff. He has unquestionably the root of the matter.

Sorry to hear that my good old friend Lily Bennett[11] is in straits. I wish I could do something for her. I have most pleasant recollections of her black-and-red bespectacled vivacity. There's no telling what I may need once the weekly gets going however—and I'll keep her in mind all right.

No! I shall retain my present work *plus* the weekly. No reward that letters has to bestow would tempt me to sever my connection with the Town and Parrish [*sic*] Councils and other Boards of which I am a duly-elected representative here. It's too funny for words—and my sense of humour must be provided for in the first place. Other things come after that.

Chris.

NOTES

1   A large town in Fife, ten miles north of Edinburgh on the north shore of the Firth of Forth.

2   Kerr's was *Porpoise Press*, the first series of which had been published in December 1922. The Press was established to publish original work in the form of broadsheets, each dealing with the work of a single author. Many of the contributors to *N.N.*— Violet Jacob, William Ogilvie, Lewis Spence, William Jeffrey, Kerr himself and (later) MacDiarmid—appeared in the series, most of which were dedicated to poetry, although there were a few issues on drama. The Porpoise Press was an important part of the new literary movement, extending the movement, not only by publishing work which would not have found an outlet, but also by re-issuing the 'Classics of

Scottish Literature', works which had become virtually unobtainable because ignored by the more commercial presses.

3   William Soutar (1898–1943), Scottish poet who was invalided for the last fourteen years of his life with osteoarthritis. He wrote in both Scots and English and published a number of volumes of poetry between 1923 and 1937. MacDiarmid edited Soutar's *Collected Poems* (Grey Walls Press, 1949) and corresponded regularly with him until his death.

4   (James) Lewis (Thomas Chalmers) Spence (1874–1955), Scottish anthropologist, writer and poet who, like MacDiarmid, was an early champion of cultural and national independence. He was an authority on the mythology of Mexico and Celtic Britain, *Mythologies of Mexico and Peru*, (1907), *Dictionary of Mythology* (1913) and was a well-established literary figure in his day. He contributed sonnets in Scots to *N.N.* 2.

5   *The Scottish Nation*, the first issue appeared on 8 May 1923.

6   The Scottish Council of the Labour Party (formed in 1915) was in the early twenties a strong supporter of Home Rule, although in later years, fighting for its political survival as a party, it was to withdraw its support.

7   The Scots National League was formed in 1921 by Erskine of Marr who was the honorary president. The league was much more fundamentalist than any of the other nationalist organisations and initially insisted upon self-government which would be completely separate from England. Later, however, it changed its policy in recognition of the need to form a strong national party and in 1928, together with the Scottish Home Rule Association, merged into the new National Party of Scotland.

8   The editorials of *The Scottish Chapbook*. MacDiarmid did write a series entitled 'A Theory of Scots Letters' (February–April 1923) in which he put forward his ideas on a cultural renaissance.

9   *See* letter 22 May 1922.

10 Robert Burns's poem of that title: 'Of a' the airts the wind can blaw,/I dearly like the West'.

11 ?Another schoolfriend from Broughton.

16 Links Avenue, Montrose.

31 January 1923

Dear Mr Ogilvie,

I am going down to East Lothian on Saturday: but returning to Edinburgh on Monday forenoon. Soutar (who writes for the *Chapbook*) and another chap are to have tea with Mrs G and I at Mackay's[1] at 5p.m. I don't know whether you can or would care to join us there: but, in any case, I shall have a few hours to spare after that (going 10p.m. train to London) so am keen to spend a bit of that time with you at any rate.

Of course you may be otherwise engaged that night. I know you are kept very busy with all sorts of things. Especially just now! I hope you have secured all the support that was necessary in re the headmastership[2]—although I could not imagine Broughton without you: and judging by the way Mackie writes some of the present studies there would be almost as much at a loss if you left them as I would have been if you had left during my first year.

Looking forward to seeing you: and hoping this finds all well at 14 St Catherine's Place.

Yours.

C M Grieve.

NOTES

1   Mackie's Tea Shop, then a popular meeting place on Princes Street.
2   Ogilvie had applied for a headmastership, but was not appointed to one until 1928.

PART FOUR

1925–1932

Biographical Summary

There is a two-year gap separating this part of the correspondence from the last section, a symptom of the fact that the contact between the two men was becoming less and less. Characteristically, MacDiarmid's renewed contact with Ogilvie concerned a job MacDiarmid had applied for as keeper at the National Galleries of Scotland. Ogilvie, generous as usual in his support for his old pupil, rallied round and tried to help him get out of Montrose. But this was to prove another failure and MacDiarmid remained in Montrose until 1929 when he moved with his family to London.

In the two-year interval which interrupted the correspondence at this point MacDiarmid had been absorbed with his periodicals, his journalism and his commitment to Nationalism. But by 1925, the date of the first letter of this section, he was preparing for publication his first three works of poetry—*Sangschaw, Penny Wheep* and *A Drunk Man*. The letters of this section trace the growth of MacDiarmid's literary reputation through Ogilvie's congratulatory responses to the various volumes as they were published and through MacDiarmid's exchange of the various reviews and commendations his works received. This section also contains the only letters from Ogilvie to MacDiarmid which have survived and these give some impression of the schoolteacher as he was in his later years, years in which he endured long periods of illness, first with his wife, and then himself. The final letter from Ogilvie is particularly touching, because it is written by a man who is aware he is close to death, yet his affection for MacDiarmid, and his pride in the fact that he had lived to see his faith in such a remarkable literary talent justified, is more than evident.

[Letterhead: *The Scottish Nation*]

February 1925

Dear Mr Ogilvie,

For some time now I have been on the look-out for a suitable job of some kind—no easy matter, for my lack of academic qualifications, the fact that I have so far as journalism is concerned served only on little local papers on the one hand and specialised on the other in forms of literature which have little or no popular appeal, and then, my politics and my expertise generally in the gentle art of making enemies have all combined to make me an adept at falling between all sorts of stools. Still, I am anxious to 'better myself'—I think that is the phrase—indeed, I owe it to my wife and daughter, if not to myself, to lose no conceivable opportunity of doing so; and some time ago I thought that, with Buchan's help, I was about to do so. But Fleet St. is in a bad way, owing to amalgamations etc. I wouldn't care but for the fact that I'm not getting any younger: indeed, I am afraid that I am getting older in some ways.

Now I've just seen an advt. which I think offers a job that would suit me. It reads;-

National Galleries of Scotland
Apptment of Keeper

Applics, are invited for the post of keeper of the Galleries. The duty of the keeper is to assist the Director in the work of the National Gallery and National Portrait Gallery, and take control in his absence. Salary £350, rising by £15 per ann. to £450 plus Civil Service bonus, which at present is £145 on the minimum, etc.

I have applied: and am whipping up all the influence I possibly can. The advt. only appeared in Saturday's *Herald*,[1] and I haven't had time yet to find out who the Trustees are. The appointment lies with them, and it occurs to me that you may know some of them or have means of getting at some of them through others. There is no forbidding of canvassing in the advt. so I am taking it for granted that it will be allowed and that it will go a long way. I shall be extremely glad if you can help me in any way.

Since I saw you last there has been little doing. I have been concentrating on foreign papers—*Les Nouvelles litteraires*[2] etc., (altho' I have an article this week in the *Scottish Educational Journal* of all places)[3]—and maintaining my *New Age*[4] stuff—and, apart from that, confining myself to Braid Scots Poetry (in which I think I am doing good work—at least Buchan[5] and others are greatly taken with it) and ultra-modern experiments in English[6] for which I cannot find a publishers and which I am not even trying to place with the limited number of periodicals which offer scope for work of that sort. As to the Scottish Renaissance useful articles have appeared on it, and my work, in the *London Mercury* and elsewhere.[7]

I sincerely trust that you are keeping much fitter than when I saw you last. Please give my kindest regards to Mrs Ogilvie, Agnes and John. We are all well here, despite a prevalence of illnesses of all kinds in the burgh.

What about trying Montrose this summer? Have you thought it over? Houses, etc, are booking up already.

I had a pleasant hour or two with Miss Manson[8] while in Glasgow lecturing to the English Assocn., and also met and am now corresponding with Miss Aitken, another old Brotonian, who is doing WEA[9] work on Scottish Literature in Greenock.

Every good wish.

Yours faithfully.

C M Grieve.

NOTES

1   The job advertisement appeared in the *Glasgow Herald* on 7 February 1925.
2   *Les Nouvelles Litteraires* was a weekly arts magazine published in Paris. It had a regular column 'La Vie Litteraire et Artistique en Province et a l'étranger' which published an article by MacDiarmid (trans by M Tirol) on the new poetry in Scotland. (20 December, 1924, p 6).
3   'Reviving the Scots Vernacular', 6 February 1925, pp 128–9.
4   MacDiarmid contributed over 100 articles to *The New Age* between 1923 and 1928 and he referred to himself as literary editor of the periodical during this time.
5   Buchan wrote the foreward to MacDiarmid's first volume of Scots verse— *Sangschaw*.
6   It is generally assumed that MacDiarmid only began his experiments in 'synthetic English' after the 1930s, but it is clear from the above remarks that he had already produced some work in that vein. His practice of including earlier works in later volumes makes it almost impossible to identify the particular poems.
7   'A Letter from Edinburgh' by David Cleghorn Thomas appeared in *The London Mercury*, November 1924, pp 89–91. It referred to the publication of *N.N., S.C., N.R.* and MacDiarmid's work in the vernacular.
8   A teacher at Broughton.
9   Workers Educational Association. Founded in 1903 by Albert Mansbridge (1876–1952) and others as an association to 'Promote the Higher Education of Working Men' and to help co-ordinate 'all working-class efforts of a specifically educational character'. It arose from university extension lectures (begun in Cambridge in 1873) which had pioneered extramural courses and continues today as a force in adult education.

The following is the first letter from Ogilvie to MacDiarmid which has survived. At the time Ogilvie was still Head English Teacher at Broughton. As usual, Ogilvie was happy to help MacDiarmid in his application for the job, but at the same time he also chastises him for a recent piece in which MacDiarmid had attacked the writer of an article on the 'Scottish Renaissance'.

67 Cluny Gdns, Edinburgh

10 February 1925

Mr dear Christopher,

You may certainly count on my doing anything I possibly can in support of your application for the post you mention. I am only sorry that at most that will be comparatively little; but once I find out who the trustees are it may turn out that I can get at some of them.

What a pity it is that you have made (as you admit) so many enemies! I especially deplored that superfluous (and for you so crude) attack on Kitchin[1]— in the *Forward*.[2] One of your enemies lost no time in throwing it in my face, and frankly I blushed for you. The mischief is that Kitchin might have been of great use to you—not to speak of his pal J C Stewart,[3] who, I fear, has been definitely alienated by the article. You took, or pretended to take, Kitchen's [*sic*] article in the *Scotsman* too seriously. It struck me as kindly enough on the whole.

I hope you have written to Dr Drummond. I am no longer a member of his church, but up to the last time I met him he never forgot to make kind inquiries about you. He is a man of wide influence, and might be of much use.

I shall let you know if I can secure any helpers.

I did not resume work till January. That night I left you at Church Hill to see my doctor was the start of a two month's illness—blood pressure and heart trouble. I am not very well yet and am glad to lie 'dormy' by the fire when I creep home from school. The others happily have only minor ailments. You do not say anything of your household health: I take it that you are all going strong. I do trust that for your own and their sakes you pull off this job or one equally good. It is high time you were out of Montrose.

Kindest regards to all.

Yours sincerely,

Geo. Ogilvie.

NOTES

1   George Kitchin (1881–1968) was a lecturer in English at Edinburgh University from
    1911–1946. A very popular figure, he had actually acclaimed MacDiarmid's
    achievement, so that the attack really was quite unwarranted and is an example of the
    way in which MacDiarmid failed to exercise some discretion. His article, 'The
    "Scottish Renaissance" Group: What it Represents', appeared in the *Scotsman*, 8
    November 1924, p 8.
2   *Forward* was a socialist weekly edited by Tom Johnston of the ILP which had been
    suppressed by Lloyd George during the First World War, but which had again taken
    up its role of 'stating clearly and plainly to the man in the street the case against
    Capitalism'. It was, therefore, a radical journal committed to destroying the old
    conservative guard and it supported the new nationalist movement in the arts, seeing
    it as pursuing identical goals. While Kitchin's article on the 'Scottish Renaissance'
    movement had been more postive than negative, he referred to the group as
    'intellectual revolutionaries' and it is clear that his own position is more to the right
    than to the left. The phrase provided MacDiarmid with a reason for attack and in the
    article referred to 'Dr Kitchen [*sic*] Moscow and the Scottish Renaissance', (*Forward*,
    22 November 1924), using the full force of his polemical style, he charged Kitchin
    with denigrating the movement, not for its poetry, but for its politics. The phrase,
    claimed MacDiarmid, implied that the new literary movement was part of a 'Great
    Red Plot' which was being directed from Moscow.
3   J C Stewart was an Inspector of Schools for the Western Division. He was possibly
    the John Christie Stewart, Classics Master at Broughton, prior to 1920.

                                                            16 Links Avenue. Montrose.

14 February 1925

Dear Mr Ogilvie,

   It is extremely good of you to respond as quickly as ever to my latest apeal for
your help. I acted at once on your suggestion and wrote to Dr Drummond. In
the meantime John Buchan has written strongly recommending me to Sir John
Findlay[1] (of the *Scotsman*, who is chairman of the Trustees), Sir D Y Cameron[2]
and Sir J M Stirling Maxwell;[3] and Professor Grierson[4] has written too to the
two-first named and also to Mr John Warrack.[5] My friend Dr Pittendrigh
Macgillivray[6] thinks I'm the last man in Scotland the Trustees are likely to
favour—and that the only thing that could make my appointment a shade more
impossible (to use an Irishism) would be any effort on his part to help me. But
one never knows. If Dr Drummond and, perhaps, Mr Wm Graham, MP,[7]
supplement Buchan's and Grierson's recommendations I may have a sporting

chance despite the fact that I have been (as I intend to remain—whatever the consequence, and they can hardly be worse than those I have already 'tholed')[8] such a 'notorious rebel'.

I was deeply concerned to hear that you have been so unwell and that you are still in such deplorably poor fettle. I earnestly hope that you may recover strength soon.

We are all fine here and Baby is thriving beautifully.[9]

Please give my kindest regards to Mrs Ogilvie, Agnes and John—all of whom I trust are well.

If I am at least lucky enough to secure an interview in connection with this job I may have a chance of seeing you ere long.

Again with all thanks.

Yours Ever.

C M Grieve.

PS   Kitchin meant kindly I know. That didn't improve matters from my point of view. I didn't take his article seriously at all—my motto being 'Speak well o' my love, speak ill o' my love, but aye be speakin''. I welcome any sort of publicity rather than a conspiracy of silence. But there was a great deal more in the matter than met the eye, and I am afraid I am impenitent in regard to the *Forward* article. I made it just as crude and vulgar as it was in the most calculating way. It may seem stupid—it certainly harms me a great deal more than it harms those I am attacking in the meantime, and it is precisely in the meantime in some ways that I can't stand much more than I've already let myself in for—but there are precedents and I think that in the long run I should count myself a more despicable failure than I am likely to be if I could recall time I had neglected for any reason whatever to bang my head against a stone-wall. But I am free of the 'cursed conceit' of considering myself right. I am not making any virtue of what I recognise as the necessities of my being.

NOTES

1   Sir John Findlay (1866–1930) then proprietor of the *Scotsman*.
2   Sir David Young Cameron, RA (1865–1945), Scottish painter and illustrator.
3   Sir John Stirling-Maxwell (1866–1956), Eldest son of the ninth baronet. He was then chairman of the Ancient Monuments Board for Scotland.
4   Herbert John Clifford Grierson (1866–1960), Scottish literary critic and Professor of English at Aberdeen, Christ Church, Oxford and Edinburgh. Famous for his influential edition of the poems of John Donne (1912) and his *Metaphysical Poets* (1921), both of which were acclaimed by Eliot.

5 John Warrack, author of several works on Greek art and scuplture. Also wrote
   Domestic Life in Scotland: 1488–1688.
6 Dr James Pittendrigh Macgillivray (1856–1938). Scottish sculptor, artist and poet.
   King's Sculptor in Ordinary for Scotland from 1921, his works include the statue of
   John Knox at St Giles, Edinburgh, the statue of Robert Burns at Irvine and the
   memorial to Gladstone in St Andrews Square, Edinburgh. Poetry—*Pro Patria* (1915),
   Bog Myrtle and Peat Reek (1922). He designed the cover of Volume II of *The Scottish
   Chapbook*. *See* MacDiarmid's appreciation of him in *C.S.S.*, pp 13–16. Macgillivray
   was right, MacDiarmid did not get the appointment.
7 William Graham (1887–1932), Scottish politician, b. Peebles. He was Labour MP for
   central division of Edinburgh 1918–31.
8 MacDiarmid's first child, Christine, was born on 4 September 1924.

The letter which follows is undated, but given the reference to *Sangschaw* it must
have been written some time after the date of the publication of that volume—9
September 1925—and before 9 December 1925, is the date of the next letter in
the sequence.

[September 1925?]

Dear Mr Ogilvie,

    I was more than delighted to hear from you. I have been often wondering
how you were: but I never write letters if I can possibly help it—I hate pen and
ink—and though I was through in Edinburgh on Friday night recently speaking
at Patrick Geddes's[1] I got no chance of running up to see you. I do hope you'll
keep on an even keel now.
    I wish you could holiday in Montrose one summer soon. I'd give a great deal
to have a few walks and talks with you. Please give my best remembrances to
Mrs Ogilvie and the children (scarcely children now). Christine is a fine
specimen of a lassie for fourteen months. She hasn't been well lately but I think
it's only her being 'among her teeth'!
    Sangschaw is only a beginning: Blackwood's have option on next two
volumes.[2] I have another half-ready.[3] I expected S. [*Sangschaw*] to meet with a
mixed reception, and it has. But the people to whose opinion I attach any
importance are unanimous. Grierson had doubts as to the validity, practicality
and desirability of what I proposed trying to do in my McDiarmid [*sic*] stuff: but
after reading *Sangschaw* he writes as follows:-
    'I have been reading it with unaffected and great pleasure. You have, I think,
succeeded in writing Scottish poetry that is quite unaffected by the Burns (no
disrespect to what is best in Burns)—Sentimental-Kailyard tradition, and which

is real poetry, imaginative and moving. One is glad to get in Scots such sincere, imaginative, musical poetry in so fine, and (for later Scotland) so surprising and fresh a strain. It makes me understand better your plea for a fresh reading of Scottish history. We have been too much 'haudin' doon'[4] by the Knox-Covenanter-Shorter Catechism tradition[5] and must recover our sense of a Scotland that was a great and prosperous country before John Knox was heard of, a country that was part of Europe in life and faith. . . . I do feel (which I do not often) that you have given me a fresh experience in poetry'.

Muir[6] has written an article on *Sangschaw* for the *Saturday Review of Literature* (USA),[7] and Saurat[8] has translated it for *Les Marges*. I am hopeful of arranging an American edition of *Annals*.[9]

I enclose for your interest an article on myself which appeared in a Border paper the other week.[10]

I am not anxious to put together my English verse—till I have some better stuff. Did you see a poem of mine some time ago in the *Glasgow Herald* entitled 'A Herd of Does'.[11] If not, I'll send you a copy.

My *Contemporary Scottish Studies* appearing in *Scottish Educational Journal* are appearing—adjusted with amplifications here and excisions there—next Autumn through Leonard Parsons.[12] I have material ready for another book on lines of *Annals*.[13] I have just written a play which I expect to have produced in Glasgow ere long. And F G Scott,[14] Professor McCance (who is art-critic of the *Spectator*)[15] and I are creating some Scottish Ballets, for which I am doing the libretti. I am writing for various papers—book-reviewing, etc. And I am to be speaking in Dundee next month, Falkirk (EIS)[16] in December and Glasgow (English Assocn.) in February.

I can't get out of Mtse. though, do what I will. And I loathe my work here. I have tried in all directions. In other respects I am far from being out of the wood. I continue—and will continue—to make enemies. I will not allow myself to be judged by anything other than the quality of my work. People who demand that in addition to doing work of a certain calibre a man must be respectable, sociable, God-fearing, compromising to meet them in one way or another, will not only find that I won't fit in, but that I will stall most violently. And my general opinions in most directions are impossible so far as contemporary Scotland is concerned. 'Determined things to destiny' must 'hold unbewailed their way'.[17]

I agree as to the difficulties a pseudonym involves one in: but I am much more inclined to give every facility for the sort of malevolence I am encountering than otherwise. I think I'll get my own back with interest in the long run. At the same time—if only to please you—I'd shed the pseudonym now, if I could—but I can't for various reasons. There are the publishers of Scott's music, etc. to consider.

How's Albert?[18] I've been looking for another novel from him. I thought a good deal of *Kirk o' Field*.

With every good wish.

Yours ever.

C M Grieve.

Of course *Sangschaw* is like the curate's egg. There's about a third of it below par, which I'm sorry I included.

NOTES

1   Sir Patrick Geddes (1854—1932), Professor of Botany at Dundee (1883-1920). A pioneer in urban planning, he also played a large part in social and educational work. Greatly influenced by Darwin, the theory of evolution pervaded his social and economic planning. He was the leader of a Celtic revival movement in the 1890s in Edinburgh and published the periodical, *Evergreen*, a journal which MacDiarmid cited as being a model for his *S.C.* Geddes's *camera obscura* was installed in the Outlook Tower at the top of the High Street in Edinburgh and this spot was a popular meeting place for various groups and arts clubs, so it is probably the Outlook Tower which is meant when he refers to 'speaking at Patrick Geddes's'.

2   Blackwood's published *Penny Wheep* (1926) and *A Drunk Man* (1926).

3   *Penny Wheep?*

4   'Held down'.

5   Grierson recognised that MacDiarmid's poetry was short-circuiting the Presbyterian tradition and was looking instead to the traditions of an older Scotland, a Scotland which through its Catholicism had enjoyed an intellectual and spiritual internationalism.

6   Edwin Muir (1887-1959), Scottish poet and critic, b. Orkney. MacDiarmid's contemporary, Muir began as a close friend and champion of his work, but they ended as literary enemies with Muir condemning the vernacular revival in his *Scott and Scotland* (1936).

7   A weekly review published in New York. Muir's article, 'The Scottish Renaissance', appeared 31 October 1925, p 259.

8   Denis Saurat (1890-1958) b. Toulouse. A French literary critic and scholar who described MacDiarmid's work in the vernacular as 'synthetic Scots'. He was lecturer in French at Glasgow University (1918-19) and later Professor of French at London University. He wrote for *The New Age* where his philosophical work *The Three Conventions* (1926) was first published. *Les Marges* was a literary magazine published in Paris from 1903 to 1937.

9   There was no American editon of *Annals*.

10 No article was retained with the letter.

11 The poem appeared in the *Glasgow Herald* on 4 April 1925 and was later published in *Penny Wheep*.

12 Published by Parsons in 1926.

13 MacDiarmid produced several short stories and prose sketches around this time which were published in various newspapers and magazines, but not published as a book. There was no production of a play by him in this period and as ballets do not have libretti it is difficult to fathom what it is he is referring to.

14 Francis George Scott (1880–1958) b. Hawick. Scottish musician and composer who set several of MacDiarmid's early lyrics to music. Scott had been one of MacDiarmid's teachers at Langholm and the contact between the two men was renewed when Scott wrote to the poet praising his work. They became great friends and Scott seems to have replaced Ogilvie as critic of MacDiarmid's work by this date.

15 William McCance, (1894–1970) Scottish painter. He was art critic of *The Spectator* from 1923 to 1926.

16 Educational Institute of Scotland, the group which sponsored the *Scottish Educational Journal* which had published MacDiarmid's *Contemporary Scottish Studies*.

17 *Anthony and Cleopatra*, III, vi, 84.

18 Edward Albert, his *Kirk o' Field* was published by Hodder in 1924.

16 Links Avenue, Montrose,
Scotland.

9 December 1925

Dear Mr Ogilvie,

I have just discovered to my disgust that I forgot to reply to you re 'O Jesu Parvule'.[1] I need not say that the *Broughton Magazine* is always welcome to anything of mine. I wrote to Scott re the music: I found that his publishers (Bayley and Ferguson) would be prepared to print you specially a copy of the leaflet with music and words to insert in the Magazine at between 2 and 3 for enough copies to cover the issue. But that would probably have been beyond the financial resources of the Mag. However, I'm afraid I'm too late now, owing to having been horribly rushed of late. I only hope you've taken my consent for granted and used the words. Excuse this hasty note. *Sangschaw* has been getting some rare reviews of late—*Glasgow Herald* (last Thursday), *Manchester Guardian* (yesterday), and *Saturday Review of Literature* (USA-2 cols).[2]

I do hope you are keeping more fit again. Kindest regards to Mrs Ogilvie and the children.

Yours ever.

C M Grieve.

NOTES

1 A lyric from *Sangschaw* which (together with F G Scott's musical accompaniment to the poem) was published in the Christmas 1925 issue of *Broughton Magazine*.
2 Reviewed in the *Glasgow Herald*, 3 December 1925, p 4; the *Manchester Guardian Weekly (Supplement)*, 4 December, 1925, p. vi; Muir's article referred to in letter September 1925?

Avondale. St Cyrus,[1]
Kincardineshire.

6 August 1926

Mr dear Mr Ogilvie,

I was greatly touched to receive your kind letter apropos *Penny Wheep*[2] published some weeks ago.

The death of one of Mrs Grieve's sisters, and a subsequent indisposition of my own, (from which I have now wholly recovered—I am really very robust despite my curious leanness) has prevented my replying sooner; these things, and the fact that I am up to the neck in proofs of *Contemporary Scottish Studies* and—worse—in rewriting, against time, (the MSS should really have been in the hands of the publishers ere this) one of the main and most difficult sections of *A Drunk Man*.[3] (Not, of course, to pretend for a moment that I am any better than ever—rather worse, alas!—in respect of my old difficulty of organising my affairs and replying to correspondence in any reasonable way. My conscience is pricking me with regard to Annand.[4] I should have written him months ago. I was so delighted with the Braid Scots number—and am so anxious that he and the others should keep to it and try it for all they're worth. But the old 'infirmity of will'—the curious inability to write—persists and worsens. It's really a side-result of far too-intense-preoccupations in other directions).

I realise fully the importance of what you urge in regard to the *Drunk Man*. It will either make or finish me so far as Braid Scots work, and Messrs Blackwood's are concerned. I dare not let them down with a work of such magnitude. As it now stands it'll be at least six times as big a book as *Sangschaw*—some risk for any publisher these days. I've let myself go in it for all I'm worth. My friend Scott, (the composer) and I afterwards went over the whole thing with a small tooth comb.[5] But we both felt that the section I've been rewriting—which comes about midway in the book and should represent the high water mark, the peaks of higher intensity, could be improved by being recast and projected on to a different altitude of poetry altogether—made, instead of a succession of merely verbal and pictorial verse, into a series of metaphysical pictures with a definite progression, a cumulative effect—and that is what I've been so busy with. It's infernally intractable material: but I've spared no pains and put my uttermost ounce into the business.[6] I'm out to make or break in this matter. There are poems in the book (which is really one whole although many parts are detachable) of extraordinary power, I know—longer and far more powerful and unique in kind than anything in *Sangschaw* or *Penny Wheep*; but that's not what I'm after. It's the thing as a whole that I'm mainly concerned with, and if, as such, it does not take its place as a materpiece—sui generis—one of the biggest things in the range of Scottish Literature, I shall have failed. Whole sections of it do go with a remendous gusto and with a sweep over a tremendous range: but there are still a few movements that want supple-ing and accelerating and bringing into harmony with the others in this way or that. So you musn't mind if I cut short this very egoistic letter.

I was glad to hear that you had again been fit, although you must have felt the strain of acting headmastership in Broughton (which I hope a happy holiday since has more than made good). I saw your name somewhere some time ago as having been placed on the list from which headmasters will be appointed and trust that ere long you will land a congenial billet. I hope Mrs Ogilvie and Agnes and John are all well. Please convey my complêments and regards to Mrs Ogilvie. I haven't had my holidays yet and do not propose taking them till the back-end when perhaps I'll go to London. In any case I'll be going down to East Lothian to my mother's for a few days and so passing through Edinburgh and will then look you up. I could fain do with a good long evening with you and a thorough talk. Each summer for the last three we've taken a house here at St Cyrus for a couple of months and, while it suits Mrs Grieve and, now, baby (who is a voracious and indefatigable little Monster) admirably it enables me to carry on my work in the dog-days with many of the effects of holidaying. But I am really feeling the need now, for divers reasons, of getting into a city and have during the past year tried to do so in all sorts of ways—but without success. I'm beginning to get desperate for I don't want to have to reconcile myself to Montrose—or the likes of Montrose—for good. But its extraordinarily difficult. However, something may turn up—and probably most unexpectedly.

Again thanking you for your welcome and most encouraging letter, and with affectionate regards.

Yours.

C M Grieve.

NOTES

1 A village five miles north east of Montrose.
2 Published 16 June 1926.
3 *A Drunk Man* is MacDiarmid's masterpiece in Scots. It was released on 26 November
   1926.
4 James King Annand (b. 1908). Then a student at Broughton and editor of *Broughton
   Magazine* (1925–6). A champion on Lallans verse (and editor of the periodical *Lallans*)
   he published the poems which accompanied MacDiarmid's letters to Ogilvie in *Early
   Lyrics* (1968). He has published several collections of poems in Scots—*Sing it Aince for
   Pleasure* (1965), *Two Voices* (1968).
5 Scott helped MacDiarmid to order the lyrics of *A Drunk Man* and claimed to have
   supplied the ending. MacDiarmid wrote that at a certain point he 'ceased to be able
   to see the forest for the trees . . . and handed over the whole mass of my manuscript
   to him. He was not long in seizing on the essentials and urging the ruthless discarding
   of the unessentials. I had no hestitation in taking his advice and in this way the
   significant shape was educed from the welter of stuff and the rest pruned away'
   (*C.K.,* p 96).
6 The preface which accompanied the first edition of *A Drunk Man* tended to play
   down the seriousness of the work, however it is quite clear from the above remarks
   that MacDiarmid fully realised the magnitude of the task and was committed to
   making *A Drunk Man* a major work.

16 Links Avenue. Montrose.

9 December 1926

Dear Mr Ogilvie,

    Many thanks for your kind and reassuring letter. I always suffer from reaction
after putting out a book: and am ridiculously sensitive to what reviewers say—
even when I know their incompetence and malice. I say to myself: what *can*
reviewers be expected to make of a thing like that *Drunk Man*—and yet I am
horribly vexed when they make nothing of it or something utterly stupid. I set
out to give Scotland a poem, perfectly modern in psychology, which could only
be compared in the whole length of Scots literature with *Tam o' Shanter*[1] and
Dunbar's *Seven Deidly Sins*[2]. And I felt that I had done it by the time I finished—
despite all the faults and flaws of my work. (At the last moment I excised lyrics
etc. which aggregated at least a third more than its published bulk). The few
people whose opinions I respect in regard to matters of this kind—i.e. who have
the knowledge and understanding of poetry in general, and of Scots in
particular—are all of like opinion to yourself, and they are isolated—scattered all
over the country and not in touch with each other. Even making a discount for

any particular partiality they share for me and my work, I think their unanimity in the matter almost proof positive that they are right. Even so the lack of interest in the book on the part of the public and the great majority of reviewers is chilling: and I am all the more glad to have a reassuring letter from yourself, and move forward again out of comparative dejection to the position that 'it is all right in its way, but will take a year or two in the nature of things to accumulate the reputation it deserves'.

I will send you a batch of cuttings in a day or two. Some of them make 'sair reading'. The sales, too, have been very disappointing so far. But then 7/6 [7s 6d] is a fair sum and times are bad. So long as Blackwood's maintain their faith, I don't care. It will be about a year at least before I ask them to publish *Cencrastus*,[3] and it may be longer. It will be a much bigger thing than the *Drunk Man* in every way. It is complementary to it really. *Cencrastus* is the fundamental serpent, the underlying unifying principle of the cosmos. The circumjack is to encircle, to Circumjack Cencrastus—to square the circle to box the compass etc. But where the *Drunk Man* is in one sense a reaction from the 'Kailyaird', *Cencrastus* transcends that altogether—the Scotsman gets rid of the thistle, 'the bur o' the world'[4]—and his spirit at last inherits its proper sphere. Psychologically it represents the resolution of the sadism and masochism, the synthesis of the various sets of antithesis I was posing in the *Drunk Man*. It will not depend on the contrasts of realism and metaphysics, bestiality beauty, humour and madness—but more on a plane of pure beauty and pure music. It will be an attempt to move really mighty numbers. In the nature of things such an ambition cannot be hastily consummated. It will take infinite pains—but along these lines I am satisfied that, if I cannot altogether realise my dream, I can at least achieve something well worth while, ideally complementary to the *Drunk Man*—positive where it is negative, optimistic where it is pessimistic, and constructive where it is destructive.

Re your little joke you were of course—professionally—my English master. I never had a Scots master. But in what I say about Scottish schools in the *Drunk Man* I am (this is my line of defence—my means of reconciling the apparent inconsistency) thinking of the effects of our Educational System on Scottish psychology in general—in my own person I am partially (for alas! I had teachers of whom I have very different thoughts than of you and one or two others) one of the very few exceptions who prove the rule.[5] Curiously the *Drunk Man* is addressed to another old teacher of mine, in my Langholm days—F G Scott [6]—we never came into contact with each other as you and I did: I lost sight of him for years: I did not know he was a composer or in any special sense a Scotsman. It was only after I began writing my McD stuff that he got into contact with me—it seemed that McD was providing the very stuff he was at his wits' end to find anywhere—he didn't know then that McD was an old pupil of his. - - - In any case, if the commentators etc. do ever descend in any measure upon my literary remains they will find ample evidence and (so far as I can gauge them) all the hows and whys of my indebtedness to you and of your exemption from the criticism I have brought against your profession as a whole of (whatever else—arguably of more consequence from many points of view—they may have done) failing to stimulate the specifically Scottish qualities of their pupils.

You do not refer to the *Contemporary Scottish Studies*. I wonder what you think of it. Clear-enough-eyed to all its faults of temper and other things (and clear-enough-eyed to the necessity too of most of these very faults if the book was to effect its main purpose) I am in no way apologetic over it. It will do its work. There was a very understanding review of it in the *Glasgow Evening News*[7]—so understanding that I think Neil Munro himself must have written it. I'll send you the cutting with the others. In other quarters of course it has been either ignored or its faults have been concentrated on in a way that partakes of the worst nature of these same faults, to the exclusion of any reference to or comment upon the real values and intentions of the book.

I also recently did the Burns selection with a provocative little preface in Benn's 6th Augustan Series:[8] and am to propose 'The Immortal Memory' at Cupar on 25th Jan., when I hope to give an address which will be the foundation of a monograph on the subject I have been contemplating for some time.

My apparent leanness is entirely due to my lack of teeth. I must really get a set of false teeth and set my friends at ease. As a matter of fact I keep wonderfully fit. I have not had a doctor since I left the Army in 1919, and no illness of any real consequence. I am frankly anxious not to die young. In many ways I am a late ripener. All my best work is still to come. I am only beginning to find myself. I have all sorts of things in contemplation—and in prose in particular and question if I will succeed in doing any justice to myself for several years yet. I have masses of stuff half-written or in rough draft that I simply cannot finish yet—at least in a fashion that will preserve my artistic integrity. But I know with the sort of intuition that guides one in these matters that it is only a question of time—I will do it yet.

You say nothing of yourself. I hope Mrs Ogilvie, Agnes, John and yourself are all well. It will be delightful indeed if you can contrive your holiday through here next summer. There is nothing I will enjoy more than a little succession of walks and sederants and talks with you. Mrs Grieve and Christine (a very rambustious little lady, indeed) are in splendid form, and join me in every good regard to all of you. Be sure and remember me to any old friend of the Broughton days—and Mackie and Annand.

With every affectionate and grateful thought.

Yours.

C M Grieve.

NOTES

1 Robert Burns's long poem in Scots published in 1790.
2 William Dunbar (c. 1460–1520). Initially a Franciscan novice, Dunbar later became secretary to a number of James IV's numerous embassies at foreign courts. His verses are among the most outstanding of the mediaeval makars and are notable for their great variety of technique and liveliness of imagination. MacDiarmid constantly directed attention to the mediaeval Scots tradition with his cry, 'Back to Dunbar', and advocated this tradition as a superior model of imitation than eighteenth century sentimental verse. *The Dance of the Sevin Deidly Synnis*, like Burns's *Tam o' Shanter*, is a fast-moving satire full of the kind of fantasy and grotesquery which features in *A Drunk Man*.
3 *To Circumjack Cencrastus*, MacDiarmid's fourth major volume of poetry. It was in fact to be four years before Blackwood's published this work in 1930.
4 'the thorn in the world's side'.
5 In *A Drunk Man* (and elsewhere) MacDiarmid attacked the Scottish system of education, which he claimed was over-Anglicised and was the main reason why Scots knew almost nothing of their own history or literature.
6 *A Drunk Man* is dedicated to Francis George Scott.
7 The review appeared on 25 November, 1926, p 2. It was highly commendatory and was unsigned.
8 *Robert Burns* (Benn). The Augustan Books of Poetry (1926), a series edited by Edward Thompson. The proposed monograph was never published.

16 Links Avenue, Montrose.

4 January 1927

Dear Mr Ogilvie,

I am enclosing all the reviews or references to the *Drunk Man* I have seen so far. I do not think any others have appeared or I'd have received cuttings or heard of them: but there will be a few to come. Neither the *Manchester Guardian* nor *Times Literary Supplement* reviewed *Penny Wheep*: but I am hoping they will not ignore the *Drunk Man*.[1] The *Irish Statesman* won't, in any case, and I expect 'A.E.' will review it there, as he did its two predecessors.[2] That's always something—to be reviewed by someone competent. Most of the Scottish papers seem to delegate reviewing to their office-boys. Surely nothing can be more hopeless than the *Aberdeen Press and Journal* man's remarks—unless it is the two or three lines in the *Glasgow Evening Times*.[3] All the same, although sales have been wretched, things are improving under the surface. I've had a sheaf of congratulatory letters from people like Professor Grierson, Dr Macgillivray, Edwin Muir etc. and I am sufficiently immodest to have no fear of the ultimate outcome.

I'm also including the only review of any consequence of *Contemp. Scottish Studies* (the others were almost unrelievedly adverse)—that from the *Glasgow Evening News*[4] which I think is pretty near the bit. It corresponds to my own view of the book.

Excuse this short note. I am also enclosing herewith a copy of my Benn *Burns*. I hope you have had a happy Christmas and New Year and that Mrs Ogilvie, the children (no longer children quite!) and yourself may have all good fortune in 1927. I am a grass-widower tonight: Mrs Grieve and Christine went off on Friday to her home and are returning tomorrow. I went to Inverness on Friday night and spent a most enjoyable week-end with Evan Barron[5] (the historian), N M Gunn[6] (the novelist) and other friends there—including Andrew Paterson[7] (probably the best artist-photographer, and international exhibitor, in Scotland), who spent most of Sunday afternoon photographing me in a variety of aspects. I'll send you one if he has got anything to satisfy him.

Yours.

C M Grieve.

NOTES

1 *The Times Literary Supplement* did, in fact, review *Penny Wheep* (24 March 1927, p 214). The reviewer (who had also revied *Sangschaw* (7 January 1926, p 8) said that *Penny Wheep* had 'the same merits as *Sangschaw* . . . a gift for seeing familiar things from new angles and illuminating poignant situations by flashes of imaginative insight'. But he did criticise MacDiarmid's incorrect usage of Scots words. When he came to *A Drunk Man* (22 September 1927, pp 650–1), the same reviewer modified his position, stating 'Mr MacDiarmid's new salvages are often strong and racy, and appear in some cases to have been drawn direct from oral sources'. As he had done previously, MacDiarmid replied to the review (6 October 1927, p 694), pointing out that his poems were in 'simple, unmixed dialect' and that he had earlier answered this reviewer and had shown 'conclusively that I was right in every instance'.

2 Reviewed by 'Gog' (pseud of Oliver St John Gogarty (1878–1957)), 8 January 1927, p 432, who described the work as 'a sustained rhapsody and at the same time a dramatic lyric of great variety and power wherein the poet is the protagonist'. 'A.E.' (pseud of George William Russell (1867–1935)), was editor of the *Irish Statesman* from 1923–30. He and MacDiarmid became great friends and corresponded over a number of years. Russell drew the sketch of MacDiarmid which appears in the *Second Hymn to Lenin*. *Sangschaw* was reviewed in the *Irish Statesman*, 3 October 1923, pp 120 (signed 'Y.O.'). *Penny Wheep* also appeared under the same signature on 14 August, 1926, pp 638–40.

3 Reviewed in the *Aberdeen Press and Journal* 27 November 1926, p 5, signed 'A.K.', and in the *Glasgow Evening Times* 25 November 1926, signed 'J.M.R.'. Both reviews were nondescript.

4   Review of 25 November, referred to in preceding letter.
5   Evan MacLeod Barron (1879–1965). He had published many histories of the Scottish
    Highlands and was also editor and proprietor of the *Inverness Courier*.
6   Neil Miller Gunn (1891–1973). Scottish novelist who had recently published his first
    work *Grey Coast* (1926) which had been very successful and which was to be
    followed by a number of novels, dealing mainly with life in the Highlands, which
    also enjoyed great popularity.
7   Andrew Paterson (1876–1948) b. Inverness. A portrait photographer of outstanding
    talent who ran *The Studio* in Inverness. Many celerities of the 1920s and 1030s sought
    him out and his portraits include those of George Bernard Shaw, Noel Coward, John
    Gielgud, Alfred Hitchcock and many others. He also made and directed a film in
    1913—*Mairi—the Romance of a Highland Maid*. His portraits of MacDiarmid are
    included in Gordon Wright's *MacDiarmid: An Illustrated Biography* (1977).

                                                            67 Cluny Gardens,
                                                            Edinburgh.

17 January 1928

Dear *Hugh* (it's shorter than Christopher),

   I feel I mustn't let more days of this New Year pass without sending on my
sincerest good wishes for the health and happiness of your little household.

   I am also anxious to hear how you are getting on, and what you have been,
are, and are likely to be, doing—not only to satisfy my own (kindly, I hope)
curiosity, but also to appease the (not so kindly, I fear) curiosity of old
acquaintances who bombard me often with enquiries about you.

   These enquiries, I may say, usually develop into heated arguments about you
and your synthetic Scots (particularly). Frankly, I fight a lone hand, tho' young
Mackie came to my aid the other night very gallantly and effectively. I hear you
are going shortly to break a lance over the wireless. I shall listen to [you] with
great interest. By the way, if it is to be from Edinburgh and you have, as on the
last occasion, an hour to spare, I shall be glad to spend it with you, and if you
have no objection bring Mackie with me. I think you will like him.

   How is the sequel to *A Drunk Man* getting on?[1] I do hope satisfactorily. And
what else have you on the stocks? I heard of your *Albion*[2] [*sic*] only the other day
and intend to get it.

   You will be interested to hear that Cassells is publishing a novel of Alberts'
next month—*Man's Chief End*,[3] it is a modern novel—a little unequal, I think,
but strong in parts. It is difficult to forecast how it will go.

I trust you are keeping fit and that Mrs Grieve and Christine are well. We are under a cloud at present. Mrs Ogilvie undergoes a major operation for *Calculus* on Tuesday first. In the circumstances you will excuse me fobbing you off with this very brief note.

Yours ever,

Geo. Ogilvie.

NOTES

1   *To Circumjack Cencrastus.*
2   *Albyn: or Scotland and the Future* (Kegan Paul) 1927.
3   Published by Cassells in 1928.

16 Links Avenue. Montrose

30 January 1928

Dear Mr Ogilvie,

I was delighted to hear from you again—but extremely sorry to learn of Mrs Ogilvie's condition. I sincerely trust that the operation was successful and that she may soon be entirely recovered. I have not had a moment to myself during the past ten days or so; or I would have written you ere this to express my concern, sympathy, and good wishes. But—busy as I have been—the matter has been constantly in my mind and I shall be glad if you can drop me a line to tell me how Mrs Ogilvie is. You do not mention yourself: but I know that this strain will have been telling upon you, and I trust that you are fit.

Alas! The BBC are restricting travelling exes. to a minimum, I fancy. At all events my last broadcast was from Dundee. I hope you managed to hear me. I am speaking—from Dundee again—in about three weeks' time on 'Outstanding Qualities of the Scots Vernacular'.[1]

You'll have seen—or heard—of course about my attack on the Burns Cult. It has received extraordinary publicity—and an analysis of press—cuttings etc. shows, to my surprise, about 50 per cent with me. I replied to Professor Bowman.[2] Mr Rosslyn Mitchell[3] and others in special articles in the *Glasgow Evening News* and *Glasgow Evening Times* last Thursday night.[4]

For the past year (since last May to be exact) I have been sending out special articles on Scottish issues and interests of all kinds at the rate of 5 columns per week through a special bureau I formed for the purpose (in connection with the Scottish Home Rule Movement):[5] These articles appeared in some 40 local papers weekly between Maidenkirk and John o' Groats—and I am satisfied that they are slowly but surely effecting a transformation of Scottish opinion.

I have all sorts of things on the stocks. *To Circumjack Cencrastus* is shaping all right—but will be a tremendous book. I do not care though it takes me a year or two. I am simultaneously working away at several volumes of lyrics— 'Demidium Anima Mea' [*sic*] (love lyrics): 'Maidenkirk to John o' Groats'[6] (purely objective lyrics—like 'Country Life'—which, you may remember, begins

> Ootside ———— ootside
> There's bumclocks bizzin' by etc.)

and 'Songs for Christine'[8] on the model of 'Hungry Waters'.

I have also been writing quite a number of lyrics in English.[9]

At the moment I am putting everything else aside to finish as rapidly as possible a little book entitled 'St Sophia: or the Future of Religion'[10] which is to appear in Kegan Paul's 'Today and Tomorrow Series'.

Albyn (which has been selling well) I am not proud of. A curious story attaches. About a year before it appeared I had written to the publishers suggesting that I should do a vol. entitled 'Caledonia: or the Future of Scotland' for their series. They agreed—and then I found I wasn't in the mood. I was too much in amongst the stuff and simply couldn't write a statement in short compass. They wrote me for the MSS several times: but I kept putting them off. Finally a period of months ensued during which I heard nothing from them. Then I happened to hear that they were announcing a book entitled *Caledonia: or the Future of the Scots* by G M Thomson.[11] I immediately wrote to them—but they said their acceptance of Thomson's book in no way prevented them accepting mine, written from a different angle—and would I send on my MSS at once? I didn't believe them—so hastily furbished up into a semi-connected form some of the stuff I'd sent out through the afore-mentioned Bureau—just a rough slapping-together of stuff written in a slip-shod and hurried fashion in the first instances. But they took it all right! And to make matters worse didn't send me galley-proofs but only paged proofs—so the corrections I tried to make would have upset the pagination and cost too much. In the finish-up I had to leave it to them to make such corrections as they conveniently could. Needless to say they contrived to make precious few and failed to make some quite indispensable ones. So that's that.

Thomson's book gave me a chance for a journalistic grand slam. I had signed articles on it in over 30 different papers (all different articles) including *Irish Statesman*, *Forward*, the *Outlook*, the *New Age*,[12] etc. etc. Quite a little feat!

I've been writing longish articles monthly too on such subjects as 'Neo-Gaelic Economics', 'Anti-Intellectualism in Scotland Today' etc. in the *Pictish Review* and the *Scots Independent*.[13]

I've been doing a lot of talking too and have a lot more in prospect—Leith on 16th Feb. (reply to Lord Sands[14] and others re 'Synthetic Scots'. Edinburgh on 17th March (Outlook Tower Club when Mr and Mrs F G Scott and myself are supplying a real high-brow programme of the latest Scots poetry, music, and argumentation).

You'll be interested to hear that Professor Saurat (who thinks I'm making a huge mistake writing in Scots) recently read my 'Moment in Eternity' to 3 American Professors at London University and reports that they were literally astounded by its beauty and power!!

Bully for young Mackie![15] I'll let you know what train I'm arriving by on 16th Feb.—on the offchance that we might have tea together (and if Mackie can come along then too all the better). I had a long letter the other week from Mrs McCuaig (Birmingham)[16]—and will be replying to her this week for sure. Delighted to hear about Albert's new novel and will be on the alert for it.

Yes—I can quite imagine that the bulk of the inquiries will be unfriendly.

People who know nothing about me and haven't read a word I've written frequently astonish my friends (also a steadily growing body) with their extraordinary animosity towards me.

A Glasgow headmaster was to give a paper at a Burns Club the other month. Another headmaster called on him the previous week.

Dialogue.

I see you're to be at —— Burns Club next week. What's your subject?
— I'm to be talking about a new poet—Hugh MacDiarmid.
— (Quick as a flash). You'll be attacking him, of course.
— No. He's not a subject for attack or defence. It's a question of whether he has any sympeance [*sic*].[17] I think he has and it's that I want to discuss.—But have you ever read any of his stuff?
— No fear!

And so the game goes on. I'm by no means tired of it.

Love to all of you and every good wish: and may 1928 (however badly it has begun) prove a happy and prosperous year for you all.

Yours.

C M Grieve.

NOTES

1   Broadcast on 14 February 1928.
2   Professor Archibald Allan Bowman (1883–1936), held the chair of Moral Philosophy at Glasgow University from 1927 to 1936. He also wrote poetry—*Sonnets from a Prison-Camp* (1919).
3   Rosslyn Mitchell (1879–1965). Labour MP who beat Asquith for his seat in the 1924 General Election.
4   On 26 January 1928, the *Glasgow Evening News* ran an article, 'Burns Worshippers Reply to Critics of the Cult', (p 5) in which the speeches given at various Burns suppers by Bowman, Mitchell, Lord Sands and others were reported. In the *Glasgow Evening Times*, MacDiarmid published his own article replying to the criticisms, 'Is Burns Immortal?', 26 January 1928, p 3.
5   *See* letter 8 January 1929?
6   'Demidium Anima Mea' [*sic*] was the title of one of the sections of *Clann Albann*, a long poem MacDiarmid started in this period, but which was never completed.
7   MacDiarmid misquotes his 'Country Life'. The opening reads: 'Ootside!—— Oootside!/There's dooks that try tae fly/An' bum-clocks bizzin' by. . . .'
8   A series of poems entitled 'Songs for Christine' was published in *Penny Wheep*, as was 'Hungry Waters'.
9   Several of the poems of *To Circumjack Cencrastus* are in English.
10 The records of Routledge and Kegan Paul show no trace of this work. The image of Sophia, the gnostic symbol of wisdom, recurs in MacDiarmid's poetry right up until the mid-thirties. He had earlier written an article, 'A Russo-Scottish Parallelism' (see *S.E.,* pp 38–43) in which he compared Soloviev's representation of Sophia with that of J Y Simpson, Professor of Natural Philosophy at Edinburgh University. *See also* 'Hymn to Sophia: The Wisdom of God', *C.P.* I, p 455.
11 George Malcolm Thomson, b. Leith, 1899, Scottish author and journalist who wrote mainly on Scottish subjects. *Caledonia* was published in 1927.
12 'Scotland and Ireland' in *The Irish Statesman*, 22 October 1927, pp 156–8, 'A Silly Book about Scotland' (signed 'L.McN.W.') in *Forward*, 26 November 1927, p 3, 'The Condition of Scotland' in *The Outlook*, 12 November 1927, pp 641–2 and 'The Truth about Scotland' in *The New Age*, 10 November 1927, pp 16–17.
13 'Neo-Gaelic Economics' appeared in *The Scots Independent*, December 1927 and February 1928, 'Anti-Intellectualism in Scotland Today' (signed 'Gillechriosd Mac a Ghreidhir') in the *Pictish Review*, February 1928. Both articles express MacDiarmid's interest in re-establishing links with the Gaelic tradition in Scotland.
14 Christopher Nicholson Johnston Sands (Title is judicial) (1857–1934). Scottish judge who was the author of several books on Scots law, history, religion and literature.
15 Mackie's *Poems in Two Tongues* was published in 1928.
16 Unidentified.
17 ?*sympathie*

The letter which follows is undated, but the reference to Mrs Ogilvie's operation and to the arrangements about meeting for tea suggests it is an additional response to Ogilvie's letter of 17 January 1928 (most probably a reply to a note from Ogilvie missing from this collection) and is likely to have been written mid or late February 1928.

Montrose:Monday

[February 1928?]

Dear Mr Ogilvie,

Alas—there's an 'if' in the business. I was speaking in Dundee on Thursday night and caught a severe chill, which bowled me clean out the following afternoon. Since then I've been in bed—and though I'm going to work today (this being a particularly busy day with me here) I'm still deplorably 'dicky'. Under these circumstances I have just written the Leith people to see if they can't postpone my appearance there for a week. If they can't, I'll come if I possibly can—but I don't want to run any unnecessary risk. I've asked the Leith people to wire me if postponement is possible. In either case I'll p.c. you on Wednesday. If I am coming this Thursday I'll travel with a train leaving here about 2 and getting into Waverley after 4—and will be delighted to have tea with you and the others.

I'm very glad to know that the operation was successful and that Mrs Ogilvie will make a rapid and complet[e] recovery.

The best.

Yours.

C. M. G.

16 Links Avenue

[Letterhead: P.E.N. (Scottish Centre)][1]

21 April 1928

Dear Mr Ogilvie,

I was sorry to miss seeing you when I was in Edinr. last—and to have been so long in writing you since. I hope that long ere this you have got rid of the troublesome 'screws' which was then afflicting you: and that Mrs Ogilvie has made an excellent and complete recovery. I have been desperately 'thrang'[2]— with all manner of irons in the fire and a difficulty in manipulating them in the congested economy of my home which has not been eased by the arrival (a fortnight ago) of a son and heir.[3] Both Mrs Grieve and he are in splendid case.

This is just a note, in passing, to show that the harassed husband and father is himself still to the fore.

I got an invitation to the Outlook Tower sent to Mackie too:[4] but he was in Crieff and wrote me a long and interesting letter. I'm going to try to get him written to today. I'd a note too—which I must answer—apropos the 'majority' special number of the *Broughton Magazine*:[5] and will of course send something before the end of May (the time-limit allowed); but what? there's a rub.

I enclose a couple of pamphlets.[6]

With kindest regards to all.

Yours.

C M Grieve.

NOTES

1 MacDiarmid had been instrumental in founding the Scottish Centre of P.E.N. in 1927 and was honorary secretary of it until 1929.
2 'busy'.
3 MacDiarmid's son Walter was born on 5 April 1928.
4 Albert Mackie was then housemaster at Morrison Academy, Crieff.
5 The Summer 1928 issue of *Broughton Magazine* celebrated its twenty one years of publication. Contributors in addition to MacDiarmid included Kerr, Mackie, Annand, Albert, Gould and Ogilvie.
6 MacDiarmid wrote numerous pamphlets in this period, many of them anonymously. One of these, 'The Present Condition of Scottish Arts and Affairs', had been published by P.E.N. recently.

67 Cluny Gardens, Edinburgh.

1 May 1928

My dear Christopher,

I had hoped to write you a decent length in acknowledgement of your gift of pamphlets and in congratulation on your achievement in the oldest creative line of all. But we are still 'in the wood' or 'in the soup' here. Mrs Ogilvie was recovering slowly but surely from her operation, and we risked going to Rothesay[1] for our Easter holiday. Unfortunately both the rooms we were in and the weather outside (it was bitterly cold all the time) did her more harm than good, with the result that she came home with a form of 'Flu' on her and has been in bed ever since. Happily there are signs today of the fever abating. You will not wonder at my silence in these circumstances.

We were delighted to hear of the arrival of the son and heir, and of the well-being of Mrs Grieve and the wee one. Christine, I fancy, will be tremendously delighted. We hope to hear of his continued progress. You, of course, with so much on hand in addition to your ordinary work need sympathy. But I have no doubt your energy (always a marvel to me) will carry you through.

I enjoyed your pamphlets and of course I have a copy of your *Albyn*, which in spite of the haste you said it was written in, reads with your accustomed fluency. Indeed I think its prose is an improvement on the involved writing of your *Contemporary Writers*.[2] Your short note gave you no opening to say how your contemplated vols. of poetry &c. are getting on. I hope satisfactorily.

I am very glad for Mackie's sake that your are including him in your list of correspondents. I have great hopes of Mackie – – –. You will have looked into Albert's *Man's Chief End*: It would be interesting to hear what you think of it. However that can wait.

By the way, I have just received from Wm Kay (an old Brotonian about your time) a vol. of clever Doggerel verse. He has been in Hong Kong for a good many years, and has been amusing his friends with parodies &c. They are very clever of their kind. You may and you may not remember him.

Speaking of Broughton. I shall take it as a great personal kindness if you are able to send a contribution, however short, to the Majority Number of the Mag. about which the Editor wrote you the other day. It will—I say this seriously, earnestly—be hopelessly incomplete unless you are represented. I am especially keen on this, as this is likely to be my last year in Broughton. I got on to a Headmaster's list two years ago and it has almost run out. It is hardly worth my while making a change, but I have my pension to think of. (Don't of course, make any reference to this in your contribution, as even yet I may be shelved).

Please accept our joint good wishes for the health etc. of your little (tho' now not so little) household.

Yours ever,

Geo. Ogilvie.

NOTES

1 A holiday resort on the Isle of Bute off the West Coast of Scotland.
2 *Contemporary Scottish Studies.*

This letter is misdated. The reference to Mrs Ogilvie's illness and to Ogilvie's forthcoming appointment suggest that is was written in response to Ogilvie's letter of 1 May 1928, the probable date is therefore 18 May 1928.

16 Links Avenue, Montrose

18 May 1929 [18 May 1928?]

Dear Mr Ogilvie,

I was delighted to see your familiar script on an envelope again, but exceedingly sorry about Mrs Ogilvie. I do trust that she may speedily be all right again.

That you should not have had a look in, as you put, for the Broughton headship after all these years of splendid service is simply awful. Man's inhumanity to man – – Scotland is simply rotten with hardship of this sort. It makes me boil – – –.

I hope the Leith school isn't too awful. But it is a great pity that without financial disadvantage at the end of the day you could not have finished your term at Broughton, but had to migrate to a different and less congenial atmosphere.

I resigned my Dundee candidature[1] simply because, while I would have polled well, I could not have come near winning, and would have spent at least £200 to £300, which—ours being a young Party—could be much more profitably spent in other directions. But my organisation will remain intact and intensive propaganda will be maintained, and on a future occasion the omens may be more auspicious. I run week-end schools there: 2 lectures, Sat. afternoon and evening: and 3 on Sunday—forenoon, afternoon, and evening.

Poetry, of course, remains my principal concern: and I am in the throes of a huge poem—*Cencrastus*. I have already written a great mass of it. But I am in no hurry. Be assured that however I may seem to be dissipating my energies, I am really working away systematically at it and fully alive to the passing of the years and determined to harvest timeously every grain that I possibly can.

I am only too willing to do what I can for the semi-jubilee issue: but what can I do? I am enclosing herewith a few new poems;[2] I wonder if they will serve. If not, please just drop me a p.c. and I will do something else. Or perhaps you could suggest something—set me a subject as in the old days—and I will promptly do my utmost to score say 70 per cent of your always far too lenient marks.

The bairns are splendid: and Mrs Grieve and myself are in excellent fettle. John and Agnes will, of course, be grown up now; I trust they are both well and doing well.

Every kind regard.

Yours,

C M Grieve

NOTES

1   MacDiarmid was to have stood as a candidate for the National Party in the 1928
    General Election.
2   No poems accompanied the letter.

The following letter is undated. The letter of 30 June 1928 refers to a
contribution for *Broughton Magazine* sent 'about 15 May', but it is unlikely to
have preceded the letter of 18 May 1928 and was probably written a few days
after this one, possibly around 20 May 1928.

[20 May 1928?]

Dear Mr Ogilvie,

    Will this serve the purpose for the *Broughton Magazine*[1] If not, please suggest
some other line I might go upon and I will do my utmost to supply something
suitable.

    Excuse this hasty note. I am infernally busy at the moment. Will you ask Mr
Douglas[2] to forgive me for not writing to him? The fact that I had not done so
went completely out of my head. I did not intend any discourtesy, and it was
very good of him to ask me to contribute.

    But perhaps you have told him I was sending a contribution—and what an
unconsciounable [*sic*] blighter I am in regard to correspondence!

    I do hope Mrs Ogilvie is now wholly recovered from that most-unfortunate
chill; and that all the rest of you are fine and fit.

    With every kind regard.

Yours

C. M. G.

NOTES

1   There are no enclosures with this letter. Selections from *Sangschaw* and *Penny Wheep*
    were published in the majority issue of the magazine, so his contribution probably
    arrived too late.
2   William Douglas, then editor of *Broughton Magazine*.

16 Links Avenue, Montrose.

Saturday 30 June 1928

Dear Mr Ogilvie,

I am dashing you off a note because I have just received the *Broughton Mag* (upon which all congratulations to all concerned—I'd have been glad to have it if only for your photograph, but, as it is, there are heaps of things to make it treasurable to me and hundreds of others)—and my article does not appear? I am wondering if you ever received it. It's quite all right if you did—and did not think it suitable, or for any other reason. I sent it to you because I wanted you to tell me (as I said in my covering note) if it would serve the purpose—and, if not, if you'd any other suggestions to make. I wondered about receiving no acknowledgement; but thought it was just because you were busy. But I spoke of it several times to Mrs Grieve and had meant to write you asking if you'd got it all right—but kept putting off doing so. I forget what I called it but it was a short essay in English and I was inordinately proud of the way in which I had turned it and of its suitability, I thought, for the end in view. Needless to say, I wrote it very much con amore—as a tribute to you, and to Broughton, and to certain dead Broughtonian friends—but alas! I'm not worrying now of course about the thing itself: but lest you should for a moment have thought me unmindful of your request. I sent it about 15th May.—In great haste, with every good wish to Mrs Ogilvie and family.

Yours. C M Grieve.

The letter which follows is misdated. The reference to 'children' (Walter was not born until 5 April 1928) and to Ogilvie's appointment as headmaster suggests that the probable date is 8 January 1929.

16 Links Avenue, Montrose

8 January 1928 [8 January 1929?]

Dear Mr Ogilvie,

I am sorry to have had to let a week or thereby elapse before replying to your letter, which I was so delighted to receive. But I am having—and likely to have for some months yet—the busiest time of my life.

But first of all, let me congratulate you on your new appointment.[1] It is strange that I missed seeing any mention of it in the papers, or otherwise hearing of it. I am delighted that this long-overdue appointment has come your way at last—although Broughton without you is unthinkable. I am glad you are taking to the change not too badly and hope you will complete your career in all comfort and happiness and good health. You do not mention Mrs Ogilvie and the children (no longer children!). Mrs Grieve joins me in wishing all of you all possible good fortune in this New Year. We are all O.K. Hard work really agrees with me extraordinarily well: and I wouldn't mind if it were twice as hard if the paths I have chosen were not so desperately unremunerative—and yet I would not, and will not, change these paths one iota. The children are fair, fat, and flourishing.

As to wider issues, I am convinced that we are going to make a big issue of our Scottish Movement.[2] The odds against us, culturally, politically, are tremendous—but a big change is taking place. For nearly two years I have been sending out three columns of propagandist matter to over 40 Scottish local papers weekly[3]—and we are now beginning to appreciate the effect. But my biggest work has been correspondence. You would scarcely credit the extent of it—the affiliations I have made all over the world—the continuous effort to knit it all up into a definite and determined movement.

I had a splendid summer holiday which did me a world of good—over in Ireland as the guest of the Irish Nation at the quinquennial Tailltean Games.[4] All the younger Irish writers are great friends of mine, and, above all, the two older figures—Yeats and A. E. You'd be interested in Yeats' opinion of my poetry. He has written to me about it in the most astonishing terms.[5] It's curious how it is making way (except in Scotland) despite the linguistic difficulty. Robert Frost,[6] the American poet, is one of the latest eulogists of the *Drunk Man*.

I had hoped to have had *Cencrastus* done ere this: but I have had too many other things to do—and besides it has developed too greatly. I have already more of it written than the bulk of the *Drunk Man*: and Edwin Muir, the only one who has seen any of it so far, is of the opinion that it is 100 per cent better than the *Drunk Man*. With luck I'll finish it this year yet: but I don't want to hurry it—it's worth taking time over.

In any case, I'll not get more done till after the election. I've a Spanish novel which I'm translating for Secker to finish:[7] and I'm committed to a book on the National Movement I want out this Spring before the election and to collaboration in another with Erskine of Marr,[8] and I've meetings to address all over the place.

By the way I've just arranged to speak for Spence[9] (along with Cunninghame Graham, I think) at Dalkeith on Saturday first. I don't know what I may be doing on the Sunday yet—I may be speaking again somewhere in the constituency—or I may go on to Inverness on the Saturday night. But if I stay in

Edinburgh overnight I should like to run up on Sunday forenoon sometime and have a talk with you if convenient.

I'm interested in all your news. I wondered what had come over Mackie.

Excuse more in the meantime. Hoping to see you, if not this week-end, soon.

And again with gratitude for your unfailing interest and every good wish.

Yours.

C M Grieve.

NOTES

1   Ogilvie was appointed headmaster of Couper Street Primary School in 1928.

2   The political movement was gathering momentum with the parties which had previously been separated coming closer together. On 23 June 1928, at a Bannockburn day celebration at Stirling, the new National Party of Scotland was inaugurated and MacDiarmid was one of the founder members.

3   Under the pseudonyms 'Mountboy' and 'Special Correspondent' MacDiarmid syndicated articles on the Home Rule Movement to numerous local weeklies between 1927–9. These articles are now located in Edinburgh University Library.

4   Named after the ancient Irish festival *Óenach Tailten*, they were held in Croke Park Dublin in July 1928 in celebration of Ireland's Celtic heritage.

5   Yeats and MacDiarmid did correspond but the letters which have survived are from the years 1934 to 1939. Yeats certainly thought highly enough of MacDiarmid's work to include a good selection of it in his edition of *The Oxford Book of English Verse*. He also sent his own work to be reviewed by MacDiarmid.

6   No article by Frost has been traced.

7   *The Handmaid of the Lord* by Ramon Maria de Tenriero (Secker) 1930. The introduction by J B Trend states that certain lines 'have been turned into a North British dialect by one who has it as *her* (italics mine) native tongue'. The lines are:

> O Death's a black, camsterrie wight,
> A sairtain cure for 'ilka ill'
> He winna tak' the lasses bright
> But leaves auld Time alane tae kill.

It seems likely that this was MacDiarmid's sole contribution to the 'translation' of the novel.

8   Ruaraidh Stuart Erksine of Marr (1869–1960). Second son of the fifth Baron Erskine, he was a founder of the Gaelic Academy, the Society of Scottish Letters and was president of the Scots National League. MacDiarmid did not publish a book with Marr, but he was contributing articles to Marr's *The Pictish Review* (*see* letter 30 January 1928). No book on the National Movement was ever published.

9   Lewis Spence and Cunninghame Graham, like MacDiarmid, were founder members of the National Party. Spence was elected vice-chairman and Cunninghame Graham, president. Spence was one of four parliamentary candidates announced by the Party.

In September 1929 MacDiarmid and his family moved to London. The editorial job with *Vox* did not work out and a number of other publishing ventures he was involved with also failed. For a time MacDiarmid was unemployed, his situation being made worse by the Depression. His lack of work, as well as other problems, put an increasing strain on the marriage and it was during this time in the south that he separated from his wife and children.

18 Pyrland Road
London, N.5.

[Typewritten—Dictated]
6 January 1930

George Ogilvie, Esq, MA,
67, Cluny Gardens, Edinburgh.

My dear Mr Ogilvie,

Many thanks for your note to hand this morning. I ought to have written you long before this but I have not become any less remiss in regard to correspondence than I have always been. My accident was a serious one and in fact I had an almost miraculous escape from death. I was thrown off a double decker motor bus and landed on my head sustaining severe concussion of the skull but fortunately no fracture. I have made an extraordinarily good recovery but must 'ca' canny'[1] for a while and avoid all mental stress and excitement, alcoholic stimulants, spicy foods &c.

I came to London in the beginning of September and have (if all goes well with *Vox*[2] as it promises to do) a very congenial and lucrative post here. Mrs Grieve and the children are with me and London is suiting all of them very well. I ought to have been here years ago and am glad that this opportunity presented itself when it did.

It may lead to still greater things. Senator Oliver St John Gogarty has been bringing special pressure to bear upon Lord Beaverbrook[3] with whom he has been staying with regard to what he considers the 'shameful way in which I have been frozen out' and I have just had an extraordinarily kind letter from Lord Beaverbrook in which he expresses the greatest admiration for my works and says that he is arranging for an early meeting. Gogarty in a letter to hand this morning, also refers to this and says that he feels that he has at last broken free 'the conspiracy of silence' which has hitherto surrounded my work.

I have all kinds of things on the stocks but the amount of work entailed in launching this new periodical and other things, have prevented my getting much done other than journalism. I am just arranging, however, with the Porpoise

Press[4] to issue a new volume of my poems early in the Spring and my big poem *Circumjack Cencrastus* (which I have spent such a long time arranging and re-arranging) is nearing completion at last and Blackwoods will publish it as soon as I can let them have the typescript.

With regard to journalism, I am busier than ever and, but for my accident, would have been appearing in all sorts of new waters. I have a special article on the Burns Cult appearing in next week's *Radio Times*[5] (which has now a circulation of $1\frac{3}{4}$ million) and I will send you a copy.

You say nothing of yourself, of Mrs Ogilvie and the children in your letter. I sincerely hope that this finds you all in the best of form and Mrs Grieve joins with me (belatedly) in wishing you all the compliments of the Season and every happiness in the New Year.

This is a short and scrappy letter but I am not up to much writing yet. I will write you a long letter soon.

Ever yours,

C M Grieve.

NOTES

1 'Be careful'.
2 The first number appeared on 9 November 1929 with MacDiarmid contributing articles under 'A.K.L.' and 'Stentor'. The periodical lasted for only three months.
3 William Maxwell Aitken Beaverbrook (1879–1964), b. Maple, Ontario. Resided in Britain and became newspaper magnate and politician. By 1930 he owned the *Daily Express*, the *Sunday Express* and the *Evening Standard*.
4 Porpoise Press had published a selection of MacDiarmid's poems in *The Lucky Bag* (Broadsheet 5, 3rd series, 1927), but no other volumes of poetry. However, they re-issued *Annals of the Five Senses* in 1930.
5 The article appeared on 17 January 1930, p 137.

In November 1930 MacDiarmid managed to get a job in Liverpool, moving there in what he thought was a temporary separation from his wife and children.

[Letterhead: 357, Royal Liver Building, Liverpool. Tel. Bank 5630]

16 December 1930

My Dear Mr Ogilvie,

I am concerned to hear of your operation and subsequent weakness and—tho' you say little about it—gather that you are still far from robust. I wish I could take a run up to Edinburgh and see you: but, alas, that is out of the question in the meantime. I ought to have written you long ere this and have frequently had it in mind to do so, but I am a procrastinating creature, a bad correspondent in any case, and for most of the past year I have been having a very rough passage, financially and otherwise. The year is closing in happier circumstances however and I have good grounds to hope that the incoming year will put me in more comfortable case. After a month or so's unemployment, following the collapse of *Vox*, I secured my present post as Publicity Officer to the Liverpool Organisation, a body run by the Corporation of Liverpool, Wallasey, Bootle and Birkenhead, to boost Merseyside interests of all kinds, and my function is to write leaflets etc. and maintain a steady flow of articles of all sorts to the home, Colonial and foreign press. It is really very interesting work and what I do is entirely dependent on my own initiative; I have to show results, of course, but apart from that I am almost entirely my own master, have an excellent office etc. The salary was not too good to start with: but I have just had a substantial rise. I am still maintaining my London home and my wife and children are there—not an ideal arrangement: but I didn't know how I'd like Liverpool, I hoped to return to London, and I didn't want to bring my daughter away from the school in London. However, we may make some other arrangement soon now. On the whole I can congratulate myself in these difficult days; there are hundreds of thousands—through no fault of their own—in a far worse plight and without such compensating interests as I have in letters, politics and other directions.

Cencrastus has its qualities and looks like establishing my name far more widely than my previous books. *The New Statesman* gave a page to it; *The New Criterion* is doing likewise; Professor Denis Saurat and Gordon Bottomley are both writing about it in the next issue of *The Modern Scot*, and Yeats has been so moved that he is writing an essay on my poetry![1] I seem to be arriving.

But I did not do in it what I intended—I deliberately deserted my big plan, because I realised I had lots of elements in me, standing between me and really great work, I'd to get rid of—and I think I've done it. My next book will be a very different matter—with none of the little local and temporary references, personalities, political propaganda, literary allusiveness, etc. It is based on Goethe's *Faust*[2] as Joyce's *Ulysses* was on Homer—i.e. takes *Faust* as its springboard—its framework—but it is to be cast in dramatic form and as straightforward and sun-clear as I can possibly make it, with none of the experimentalism and ultra-modernist elements Joyce used. But we'll see. I'm working very hard on it and hope—although it's an enormous proposition—to have it ready for publication this Spring!

My kindest enquiries regarding Mrs Ogilvie and your children—children no longer. I hope they are all well. Please remember me kindly to any other friends with whom you may be in touch. I see a good deal of Kerr here; he is very comfortably fixed, with a nice home, and a good Scots wife and a delightful little boy—and your name frequently crops up (always with great gratitude to you) when we foregather.

You may be sure that if and when I am in Edinburgh—or, more probably, Glasgow but with a chance of popping through to Edinburgh—I'll not lose the chance of seeing you; I would give a great deal for a long crack with you. May the opportunity come soon!

The best of Christmas wishes to you and yours and may 1931 be a happy year for all of you, and,—first and foremost—see you speedily and completely recovered from the after effects of your illness and operation.

Ever yours.

C. M. G.

NOTES

1 *To Circumjack Cencrastus* was published by Blackwood's in 1930. G M Thomson's review, 'A Star in the North Sky', appeared in *The New Statesman* on 6 December 1930, pp. xxiv–vi, and he described the work as 'a tantalising, beautiful, exciting and irritating book'. Edwin Muir's laudatory review appeared in *The New Criterion*, October 1930, and the two reviews by Saurat and Bottomley (again, both laudatory) appeared in the January 1931 issue of *The Modern Scot*. As far as can be determined, Yeats wrote no essay or review of MacDiarmid's work.

2 This work never materialised but MacDiarmid's interest in doing a book based on Goethe's *Faust* may have stemmed from the friendship he was developing with Barker Fairley in those years. Fairley (b. Barnsley, Yorks, 1887) is an authority on Goethe and MacDiarmid had corresponded with him about his book on Doughty, *Charles M Doughty: A Criticial Study* (1927).

When MacDiarmid moved back to London in 1931 his family problems came to a head and his marriage to Margaret Skinner ended in divorce in 1932. In 1931 he met Valda Trevlyn whom he subsequently married. In 1932, together with Valda and their young son Michael, he returned to Scotland. The family lived at Longniddry, near Edinburgh, for a short time before they moved on. By late 1932 Ogilvie was very ill and, as the letter which closes the correspondence suggests, was aware that he had little time left. Despite his own extreme difficulties MacDiarmid kept up his contact with Ogilvie and visited him in the months before his death.

67 Cluny Gdns, Edinburgh.

31 October 1932

Dear Christopher,

It was with great pleasure my eye fell the other morning on an envelope with you chirography—'loved long since but lost awhile'.[1] Indeed I had come to think of it as lost altogether, and had added it to a sadly growing list of memories. Of course, as one gets old he is thankful, amid his accumulated losses, that memories at least are left him, and that they brighten as they lengthen. And tho' it appeared I had lost you and your occasional letter, your memory would always be, I know, among those that 'glow and glitter in my cloudy breast'.[2] Hence my shock of pleasure when your letter made it clear that I had been premature in so coming to think of you.

I would have made an attempt, too, I daresay, to get into touch with you after my long illness and convalescence, but I learned you had left the last address of yours I had, then my wife's long ordeal engrossed all my thought and leisure. And though I have lost her, I have now thanks to that and the dregs of my operation so small a margin of energy left that I have little heart to search for lost threads.

I ought of course to say that I have been following you, with undimmed interest, in your poetry, and I was touched by your great kindness in sending me a copy of your 'Second Hymn to Lenin'.[3] I am glad to see that you [are] keeping at it, in spite of the dead set that our mandarins are still making against you, with of course most notable exceptions—so notable indeed that the others don't really count, though one grudges them their spiteful power to deliver and damn with at best faint praise.[4]

It was a double pleasure to learn that you are to be so near for a time, and I am looking forward to an occasional chat with you—and with all the good will in the world to Mr Lawson[5]—all by ourselves. Any time from 3.30 daily and all day Saty. and Sunday is yours for the asking. I can meet you somewhere in Princes St. or await you here any evening or any hour on Saty. or Sunday.

Ever yours

Geo. Ogilvie.

NOTES

1　From John Henry Newman's 'Pillar of the Cloud':

　　　And with the morn those Angel faces smile
　　　Which I have loved long since but lost awhile.

2   Quotations unidentified.
3   Published in *The Criterion*, July 1932, pp 593–8.
4   Alexander Pope's 'Epistle to Dr Arbuthnot': 'Damn with faint praise, assent with civil leer.'
5   Unidentified.

In 1933 MacDiarmid moved with his new family to Whalsay in Shetland where he remained in virtual isolation and in extreme poverty for the next ten years. On 31 March 1934 George Ogilvie died. He is buried in Morningside Cemetery in Edinburgh.

INDEX

Works of Hugh MacDiarmid are listed under Grieve, Christopher Murray: 'Works'. Published works are italicised. Poems, broadcasts and articles are enclosed in speech marks. Other works mentioned were unpublished.